MICHAE

COACHING
POSITIONAL
SOCCER

Perfecting Tactics and Skills

Meyer & Meyer Sport

British Library of Cataloguing in Publication Data
A catalogue record for this book is available from the British Library

Coaching Positional Soccer
Maidenhead: Meyer & Meyer Sport (UK) Ltd., 2021
ISBN: 978-1-78255-214-7

© 2021 by Meyer & Meyer Sport (UK) Ltd.
Aachen, Auckland Beirut, Cairo, Cape Town, Dubai, Hägendorf, Hong Kong, Indianapolis, Manila, Maidenhead, New Delhi, Singapore, Sydney, Tehran, Vienna
 Member of the World Sport Publishers' Associatoin (WSPA), www.w-s-p-a.org
Printed by Print Consult GmbH, Munich, Germany
Printed in Slovakia

ISBN: 978-1-78255-214-7
Email: info@m-m-sports.com
www.thesportspublisher.com

CONTENTS

ACKNOWLEDGMENTS

I thank my parents, Bill and Willow, for having the courage to send me across the country to a three-week soccer camp at the age of 12. This experience was life-changing and set me on a path not often experienced by children raised on a farm in rural California. Their enduring support and encouragement have been essential to all my life accomplishments.

My wife, Abigail, not only put up with this childhood passion, but along the way helped develop and run a premier soccer club, drove our children to countless soccer events, and took over all essential home responsibilities while I finished the book on weekends and evenings. She set the bar very high for any soccer mom.

I would also like to thank my in-laws, Seth and Charlotte Singleton, who have hosted our family in the Bahamas over the past three years, where so much of this book was conceived, written, and edited. I am especially indebted to Charlotte's detailed and expert editing of the manuscript, which greatly improved the clarity of my writing.

My development as a youth player was only possible by the coaching, mentoring, teaching, and friendship of local soccer coaches Jim Pfaff, Eddie David, and Dennis Olsen. Hubert Vogelsinger filled out my soccer education with "perfect skills" and essential life lessons.

The creation of the book was also a result of the support of Meyer & Meyer, who understood the vision behind it. Academy Soccer Coach provided the software for the diagrams and was quick to respond to all questions. Raina Taseva's sympathetic and detailed sketches brought the manuscript to life.

INTRODUCTION

QUESTION #1:
"HOW WOULD YOU SCORE THE PERFECT GOAL?"

Imagine your team wins the ball. A defender then plays the ball back to the goalkeeper, who looks up and scans the field. What does your goalkeeper see, and where is the first pass made? If you wanted your team to score the ideal goal, what would happen next? Can you imagine all your players' initial movements when the opponent applies light pressure to the defense, versus moderate or heavy pressure? What are the skills required by the players after the goalkeeper plays the ball out? A variety of tactical movements and individual skills will provide the scaffolding to carry the ball directly and quickly, or indirectly and patiently, up into the midfield where more choices await. Does your team patiently probe, trying to set up high-percentage attacking opportunities? Or does it skip directly to attack, which can be done centrally or through wide positions, by dribbling or passing?

First, you need the ability to see the game played out in your mind before you can effectively coach your players. This visualization exercise can reveal your level of understanding of the game. If you struggle to identify the specific tactics and skills required to bring the ball forward under various circumstances, then this manual will be helpful to you regardless of the level of soccer you coach. This manual was written to help both novice and elite coaches create practice sessions that improve their players' tactics and skills so that their teams can play in a modern, adaptive, and effective style.

Designing a practice plan can be difficult because soccer is challenging to understand and thus difficult to teach. The fluidity of the game, combined with a large assortment of skills and fitness requirements, can confound the coach. Practice planning is especially difficult in light of the conflicting needs of meaningful repetition to solidify learning and variety to ensure team development and adaptability.

Just as a cathedral can be built of individual bricks with the right blueprint, a sophisticated soccer style can be developed by learning singular skills and tactics organized together in a complex design. Brick by brick, skill and tactic by skill and tactic, your team can learn to play an advanced style as displayed by your favorite professional and national teams. Though mesmerizing, when broken down into bite-size units, even Barcelona's passing style can be understood and taught to your team. Soccer has a certain mystique, but it is not unfathomable once you understand the phases of play, coaching elements, and player principles. Focusing your coaching on these core building blocks will make it easier for players to learn what they need to accomplish during a game, whether defending or attacking.

The coaching approach of this book is "positional" because players are expected to frequently change their positions to dominate the fluctuating spaces on the field. This manual will help you ensure that your players develop diverse skills and tactics, allowing them to better adapt to the rapid changes within a game and be capable of playing multiple positions. The "universal player" is an essential component of a modern team (Whitehouse 2014).

AN ANSWER TO SOCCER'S COMPLEXITY: "PUT A BOX AROUND IT"

The insights for this book came from an assortment of learning experiences, including analyzing soccer games. One thought experiment I conduct regularly is to freeze a game in my mind and put imaginary cones around the game play to mark out a pretend practice field. Then I ask a series of questions:

"Where on the field is the play?"

"What players are within the practice field?"

"How many players are involved?"

"What is the objective of the team's play?"

"What problems are the players trying to solve?"

"What skills and tactics are used to solve the problem?"

"What type of endurance, speed, strength and agility are needed to solve the problem?"

"How does one transition to the next play?"

"Can other problems or solutions occur in the same area of the field?"

"What happens if the players fail at solving the problem?"

This mental exercise has helped reveal the underlying structures and dynamics of top teams.

STYLES OF PLAY: PLAN B

"It's always harder if you are forced to play through opponents rather than to concentrate on the transition."

–Jurgen Klopp (Honigstein 2018, pg. 268)

A style of play can be defined as the team's general approach to moving the ball from one end of the field to the other, along with the team's approach to defending. The complexity of the game allows for multiple styles of play. A team can play long or short, defend high or low, swarm or sit back, play quickly or patiently and still be successful. Some approaches are better in certain circumstances—for instance, counterattacking teams can do better against teams that push many players forward to retain numbers around the ball, but leave open space behind them.

A style of play can thus cut two ways—perfecting ways to play well in some circumstances but making a team potentially vulnerable in other circumstances. Although a distinct style of play can help a team achieve success, it can be argued that a style of play can be potentially limiting at times and that an even better goal is to have styles of play—a viable Plan B or even Plan Bs. A Plan B is an alternative way for the team to attack and defend that is different from their dominant playing style. Assimilating a wide variety of skills and tactics makes a team less predictable and more able to adapt to their opponent's strengths and weaknesses.

A PLAYER'S GAME

"The influence that the coach can exercise on players during a match is really very limited. That's why I teach players to think for themselves and to subjectively make judgements."
–Guus Hiddink (Meijer 2006, pg. 97)

"A good footballer is somebody who can offer the perfect solution in an unpredictable situation."
–Arsene Wenger (Honigstein 2015, pg. 211)

Coaching styles can be divided between those focusing on the game's flow (e.g., motivators) and those that focus on the game's structure (e.g., tacticians or strategists). However, during a soccer game it can be difficult for a coach to motivate or organize a team, given that soccer has few natural breaks during which coaches can speak directly to players, games are long in duration, play is fluid and unpredictable, and games are played over a large area. A soccer coach's inability to directly influence a game once it has started is why soccer is often described as a player's game. The best strategist cannot plan all the players' movements, and the greatest motivator cannot shout instructions on every play. Once the game begins, players must make split-second decisions on their own.

This manual explains the key principles that players need to use to solve problems in the game. Players who learn these principles will be less dependent on coaching strategies or sideline direction.

"My two qualities were great technique and insight, which happen to be two things you can't measure with a computer."
–Johan Cruyff (Meijer 2014, pg. 255)

QUESTION #2:
"IF YOU WERE WATCHING A TRYOUT FOR 10-YEAR-OLD PLAYERS, WHAT DO YOU THINK WOULD BE THE NUMBER ONE DETERMINANT OF FUTURE SUCCESS FOR THESE PLAYERS?"

Typical answers would include athleticism (strength, fitness, speed), skill level (dribbling, passing, shooting), and mentality (competitiveness, leadership, game intelligence). It has become clear from research and experience that none of these traits can perfectly predict which youth player will be most successful. One reason that predictions are so poor is that children change so dramatically through adolescence in their athleticism, attitude, coordination, and skill level. There is another factor, perhaps not stressed enough, which is not related to the qualities or experience of the players, but instead to the quality of the child's coaching.

The essential role of coaching in a player's development could be a primary reason why soccer scouts can struggle to pick the next great player, since so much of player development depends on the abilities and attributes of the player's future coaches. The importance of coaching is not limited to youth development. Even top professional players can show improvement or have sudden downturns when exposed to different styles of coaching.

Although it can take time to learn, with patience and perseverance and even with limited soccer experience, you can master the ways to coach that give each player the chance to achieve full potential.

CHAPTER 1

PHASES OF PLAY, COACHING ELEMENTS, AND PLAYER PRINCIPLES

Your team's tactics will be dictated by the type of challenges faced by your team at different points of the game. The primary tactical challenges are described here as "phases of play." There are three distinct phases of play when in possession of the ball: building up, probing, and attacking, and two phases when defending: block-zonal defending and pressing. The challenges of each phase of play are solved by specific playing styles taught as "coaching elements." Each coaching element provides a unique solution to overcome the tactical challenges of a phase of play. The coaching elements are taught through "player principles" that describe the specific tactics and skills essential to each coaching element.

PHASES OF PLAY: TEAM CHALLENGES

"The space on the pitch is the essential factor."
–Johan Cruyff (Cruyff 2016, pg. 267)

Practice planning is organized around the phases of play. These phases of play present unique challenges that teams must solve in a soccer game and are dictated by where the ball is on the field. For example, moving the ball from the team's defensive half into the midfield is a different challenge than keeping possession of the ball in the opponent's half, which is typically more crowded with opposition. Creating chances for a goal poses its own unique set of problems to solve. By understanding these tactical challenges, you can design your team's practices with a more nuanced understanding of the game. There is no "one shoe fits all" scenario with coaching soccer—very specific practices need to be created to address the unique dynamics of each phase of play.

The three phases of play that occur when a team has the ball are dictated by the changes in circumstances as the team advances up the field, where a higher technical ability is required as space tightens and a faster speed of play is required. The defending phases of play are defined by where the team is trying to win the ball—in the opponent's defensive half through pressing or in their defensive half with block-zonal defending. Descriptions of each phase of play are presented here.

PHASE OF PLAY #1: BUILDING UP

"Bring the ball out well, and you will play well."
–Pep Guardiola (Winter 2014, pg. 119)

"The aim was to create numerical superiority to win the ball, then spawn out, like a fist that opens."
–Wolfgang Frank (Honigstein 2018, pg. 57)

In build-up, the challenge is to move the ball forward within a space that is too far away from the other goal to score or set up an attack directly, but can be made very large when players "spread the field" and stretch their opponents from side to side and front to back. In other words, while the team in possession is at a disadvantage because it cannot apply direct pressure on the other team's goal, at the same time it has the advantage of large areas of space available for play.

The team in possession has room to run into space to receive a pass, dribble and pass away from pressure, and often has more time on the ball than in other areas of the field. Player movements and touches on the ball must be precise and predictable. With all the space, there is little need for riskier dribbling and passing that can more easily go wrong. Well-rehearsed and inherently-safer supportive positioning, checks (a sudden and quick dash) to the ball, and protective half-turns across the body will be the more reliable means to advance the ball into the midfield.

PHASE OF PLAY #2: PROBING

"The basic idea is to set up camp in the opposition's half."
–Juanna Lillo (Perarnau 2016, pg. 86)

Probing becomes necessary when the attacking team cannot directly attack the goal after bringing the ball up to the halfway line. Probing is the only phase that is optional—and thus sometimes skipped over in training.

The goal of probing is to move the ball quickly around in the opponent's half until an attack on goal can be created. Players in the probing phase are under pressure and in tight areas of the field. Players use either one- and two-touch passing or unsuspected turns to unsettle and disorganize defenders. Whereas in the build-up phase the possessing team will make the field as large as possible, in probing the attacking team will need to bring several players around the ball to ensure numerical superiority—while still keeping a player wide to provide an escape from the pressure.

PHASE OF PLAY #3: ATTACKING

"When in doubt, go back to basics: Attack, Attack, Attack."
–Pep Guardiola (Winter 2014, pg. 84)

In build-up, the challenge is to use the large space in the defensive half to safely move the ball up to the halfway line. In probing, the challenge is to keep possession of the ball while under pressure and in tight spaces in the opponent's half. In both situations, the team challenges (i.e., phases of play) are defined by how the opponents pressure the attacking players with the ball. The team in possession must now assert themselves by attacking spaces between them and the defenders by dribbling or passing.

PHASE OF PLAY #4: DEFENDING

Defending is a phase of play that focuses on protecting the goal. The defensive approach is generally based on whether the team seeks to win the ball in their defensive half or in the opponent's half.

BLOCK-ZONAL DEFENDING

---

*"So that was (98 World Cup winners) France's back four defenders.
Solid, tight and well-disciplined."*
(Gray 2000, pg. 261)

Block-zonal defending typically occurs in the team's defensive half and consists of two groups of three to five players—a midfield line in front of a defensive line. The aim is to squeeze the space around the ball with defenders in tight formations. The limited space around the goal allows the defending team to mark areas of the field rather than just individual players, since the defenders know where the attackers are headed (i.e., the goal). Defensive players in lines shift side to side and up and back to stay in front of the ball and block dribbling and passing lanes to the goal. Individual players step up to pressure the ball before dropping back when the ball has been passed.

PRESSING

"We need to go step by step, all of us in unison. Lose the ball and—pam!—we win it back quickly because our positional play has us all tightly linked."

–Pep Guardiola (Winter 2014, pg. 231)

"Gegenpressing being 'the best playmaker'."

–Jurgen Klopp (Honigstein 2018, pg. 224)

Pressing typically occurs in the opponent's half while they are trying to build up. If the pressing players fail to win the ball back immediately, there is little threat of the opposition creating an immediate attack on the goal. Defenders need to be organized in block-zonal defending, whereas pressing players sprint about trying to catch the opposing team off guard and win the ball deep in the opponent's half, where one or two passes can lead to a shot on goal. To press in such a large area, players need to swarm as a pack, create pockets to funnel play, and put pressure on the ball while simultaneously cutting out passing angles.

COACHING ELEMENTS

"They broke football down into its constituted parts: the small movements, right positioning, the concentration needed to control and play a ball properly."

–Matthias Sammer, German FA (Honigstein 2018, pg. 146)

"It is a type of attack that needs structure and continuous geometrical formations; triangles, rhombus etc. This is why it is positional, because we need the combination of various players in specific tactical positions in order to accomplish it."

(Basile 2015, pg. 15)

"Our players had four reference points: the ball, the space, the opponent, and their own teammates. Every movement had to happen in relation to these reference points. Each player had to decide which of these reference points should determine his movements."

–Attributed to Arrigo Sacchi

The eleven coaching elements are the essential tactical lessons that should be taught to your players. The coaching elements provide your team with a cohesive set of skills and tactics to solve the problems posed by each phase of play. Each phase of play has a variety of solutions. Your team's "style of play" results from the particular coaching elements used to solve game challenges. The specific skills and tactics introduced in each coaching element are listed in the practice plans in chapter 5 and summarized in the appendix.

The style of play best suited to the build-up phase is dictated by the type of pressure of the opponent's team on the defensive backline, which can be described as light, moderate, or heavy:

- With light pressure, the optimal strategy is to work the ball back and forth from side to side, safely easing forward around the pressure.
- In moderate pressure, the opponent will push additional players forward, leaving more open space in the middle of the field to play through.
- Under heavy pressure, when the opponent commits players forward to press both the defenders and midfielders, the best option can be to pass directly to the forwards, who will have space in front of them to receive the ball.

Probing, which involves keeping possession of the ball in the defending team's half in order to set up attacking opportunities, is accomplished either by:

- surrounding the ball with several players and using short passes to keep possession near the opponent's goal, or
- creatively turning to get free of pressure.

These two approaches often occur rapidly in succession, because quick passing puts a player in a position to make a sudden turn that creates the space needed to pass or to dribble forward.

Goal-scoring opportunities can be created from 1v1 dribbling, combination passes, through balls, crosses and counterattacks. As in the build-up phase, the type of attack most likely to create goal-scoring opportunities will depend on the way the opponent defends:

- An opponent who keeps the defenders up closer to the halfway line is more vulnerable to the through ball.
- Teams that keep their players close together (i.e., narrow) will be more vulnerable to wide play and crossing.
- Teams that drop off and defend with most of their players positioned close to their own goal are more vulnerable to combination passing.
- Teams that push many of their players forward into the opponent's half to press are vulnerable to counterattack.

Defending requires flexibility in different game scenarios:

- Teams can drop back in a block-zonal defense when defending in their half to reduce the amount of open space in front of their goal.
- To set up quick chances to score, teams can press the opposition to win the ball in the opponent's defensive half.

PLAYER PRINCIPLES

"Transform 'know-how' into a 'knowing about know-how.'"
–Vitor Frade (Tamarit 2014, pg. 56)

"You play football with your brain...If you just play intuitively, you perform your tricks at the wrong moments."
–Louis Van Gaal (Meijer 2014, pg. 63)

"Football is played with the head. Your feet are just tools."
–Attributed to Andrea Pirlo

The "phases of play" describe the problems that need to be solved based on the positions of the players and the ball on the field. The "coaching elements" describe the solutions to these phase challenges, and the "player principles" represent the essential concepts players need to understand to make the right decisions on the field. Players are taught these principles so they know why they should use certain tactics or skills in a particular drill. This insight will make it easier to later apply the learning to the actual game environment. These player principles are listed in the practice plans in chapter 5 and summarized in the appendix.

CHAPTER 2

THE ESSENTIALS OF PRACTICE PLANNING

"(The coach) must recognize the team tactic aspect, analyze it, make it trainable in an exercise that makes that team tactical aspect come to life."
–Rinus Michels (Michels 2001, pg. 29)

"My secret is practice."
–David Beckham (Syed 2010, pg.62)

PRACTICE PLANNING: AN INTRODUCTION

Teams will play as they practice, so practices need to mimic the actual game as much as possible while still honoring the need to break the game into parts for ease of learning. The "unbreakable entirety" of the game will not be forgotten in practice if you ensure that all elements of the game are included during each drill (Tamarit 2014, pg. 21).

Tactical, technical, psychological, and physical components are typically expressed together in soccer game moments. When a player dribbles to make a crossing pass to a teammate, the acts of dribbling and passing are skills that are used within a tactical strategy, say, a run behind the defense. The sprinting of players to get to the cross is a physical requirement, and the mindset to beat the defender to the ball is a psychological component. Coaches need to ensure these four components are addressed and encouraged in every drill, even when the drill focuses more on one component than another.

The learning objectives of a practice should correlate with specific game requirements. Even popular two-touch passing drills are not always tactically specific enough to generalize to the game. For example, only allowing players to use two touches in an attacking drill can prevent players from practicing 1v1 dribbling.

A practice plan guided by a cohesive tactical vision will have a bigger impact on player learning. Practice drills that are not connected and do not have an overarching plan are much less effective. The specific tactical orientation of the practice knits together the skills and tactics so they can be more easily reproduced in the game.

THE PRACTICE PLANNING DILEMMA

There are two competing processes at work when designing a practice plan. The first is the need to teach players specific tactical lessons and technical skills, and the second is the need to keep a sense of the game's continuity intact. If coaching overemphasizes one side or the other, the practice's effectiveness will be reduced, and your team will not achieve its potential. For example, when a practice is mostly structured around learning specific tactics or skills, then players do not learn how to quickly and correctly adapt to constantly changing game challenges. On the other hand, coaches who focus mostly on game play will not provide their players with the appropriate training to perfect a variety of essential skills and tactical movements.

A practice plan should be structured to balance "whole-learning" with "part-learning" so players can effectively play in a variety of styles in a game.

A TEMPLATE FOR PRACTICE PLANNING

"Tactical behavior is not like riding a bike, unfortunately. You have to practice again and again."

–Jurgen Klopp (Honigstein 2018, pg. 88)

To ensure players can develop a whole-game understanding and improve specific tactics and skills, I recommend that practices be divided into three main sections: the warm-up game (consolidation), technical and tactical development (acquisition), and the ending standard game (incorporation). Since the players' feel for the continuity of the game should be a priority at every practice, it is important that an actual soccer game begins and ends the practice.

PRACTICE PLANNING SECTIONS

1ST SECTION: WARM-UP "CONSOLIDATION" GAME (15-20 MIN)

Practices should start with a game—a game with standard goals and positions. In this warm-up game, several important objectives are accomplished. First, the team is given a fun activity that motivates players to show up for practices on time. Second, this warm-up game offers an opportunity to reinforce previous learning, so earlier tactical and technical development is not forgotten. Lastly, playing the game helps develop in players a sense of how the parts of the game are integrated. We practice to play the game, which is fluid and dynamic and requires constant transitions and adaptations. During this game, I suggest that you use the "CPS Team Progress Rating Form" found in the appendix to assess the team's development.

The warm-up game is focused, structured, and active. Nothing new should be taught in the initial game. The lack of formal coaching will make the game more fun and allow players to be more expressive.

2ND SECTION: SKILL AND TACTICAL DEVELOPMENT "ACQUISITION" STAGES (40 MIN)

In the second or middle section of practice, the focus is on teaching new skills and tactics. The best method for teaching a complex skill and tactic is for the player to initially learn in a low-pressure environment and gradually perform the skill and tactic under increasingly more pressure. Incremental loading of pressure helps build confidence and ensures skill and tactical learning can be applied in an actual game. Step-by-step instructions on how to incrementally add game-like pressure to drills can be found in the appendix.

There are three essential stages of skill and tactical learning. Each stage has unique fitness and psychological components.

STAGE 1: PERFECTING SKILLS AND TACTICS

In the first stage of technical and tactical development, the essential skills and game movements are learned and rehearsed without pressure from an opponent or pressure to score a goal. The specific body positions for each skill can be isolated to improve player learning through neuromuscular training. It is important that you or an advanced player demonstrate the drills the correct way. Any deficiencies in skills and tactics not resolved at this point in the training will typically get worse as game pressure is increased. Be both patient and insistent at this stage of training to ensure player development. There is no shortcut to perfecting technique. It can be helpful at this stage to have more than one coach in the practice area so that all players get enough attention. Vary the drills to keep players engaged.

At the end of the drills that focus on perfecting skills and tactics, a simple competitive game can be introduced that links this stage with the competitive games in Stage 2. This game can reveal how well players have learned the skills and tactics and is also a fun reward for their hard work.

PSYCHOLOGY

"Practice, practice, practice" is your mantra, as your players need to perform skills and tactical movements repeatedly to ensure they develop perfect technique. The lack of competition in these drills can reduce player fun. The coaching challenge of Stage 1 is to instill in players the motivation to do repetitive exercises with full energy and focus.

FITNESS

Stage 1 drills should focus on agility and sprinting form. Begin this stage with agility drills that prepare the player for specific skill and tactical exercises. For example, ladder work is effective at helping players improve their ability to learn dribbling moves, and zig-zag running drills are a useful introduction to defending practices which require changes of direction. Player speed can be improved in drills that require quick changes in position from one line to the next.

STAGE 2: COMPETITIVE GAME

Next, players will use these essential skills and tactics under pressure from an opponent—but often without a standard goal as a target. Competitive games are generally small-sided, so players have ample opportunities to practice what they have just learned. Since these games tend to be inherently more fun and game-like, they require less variety than skill drills in Stage 1.

PSYCHOLOGY

Small-sided competitive games are an ideal time to discuss the psychology of winning and losing—how to identify with the effort but not the result. While there are winners and losers in games, no player is an actual "loser." You want to be appropriately supportive with players who seem to take losing too personally.

FITNESS

Three-to-five-minute small-sided games improve a player's conditioning. The intensity is high for the duration of the drill, which improves player readiness to perform high-energy work for an extended amount of time.

STAGE 3: POSITIONAL GAME

In Stage 3, the positional game should be performed on half a standard-sized soccer field. Typically, this stage will involve the attackers playing against the defense toward a goal, with the defending side scoring by passing the ball through small goals. The Stage 3 exercise is a crucial step toward helping players integrate what they've just learned. If you cannot help your team improve at finding opportunities to perform specific skills and tactics in a Stage 3 exercise, then it is unlikely your team will generalize the skill to the standard game.

You may consider doing Stage 3 positional games that first have the attacking team play toward an end zone before playing to score on a standard goal. In an end zone game, a team scores by passing or dribbling into a marked-out area rather than shooting on a goal. The end zone game allows your attacking and defending teams to play in standard formations, but without the added dynamics and pressure of scoring on a standard-sized goal.

PSYCHOLOGY

Stage 3 is the litmus test for your team to demonstrate whether the skills and tactics learned in the previous two stages are good enough to be used in a standard game. Players need to separate foreground, i.e., the dynamic play occurring right around them, from the background, i.e., the movements of the other players and the position of the goal. For example, players can create the perfect wall pass without seeing that the best option at that moment is not to pass but to shoot on goal, an option that is open directly in front of them.

FITNESS

Stage 3 drills require players to play on a standard field, which is typically much larger than the playing area used in small-sided games. Players will run longer distances at faster speeds. Short periods of game play will introduce your team to the physical requirements of a standard game. You can increase the intensity of the drill by having players sprint back into their starting positions at the start of every new play.

3RD SECTION: STANDARD "INCORPORATION" GAME (25 MIN)

The practice ends, as it began, with a standard game. By the game's conclusion, your team should be able to demonstrate how they combine new learning with previously taught skills and tactics to expand their playing ability.

PSYCHOLOGY

An important aspect of the final game is the focus on transitions between attacking and defending. Players must be mentally focused in order to transition quickly and correctly. For example, it is not uncommon for players to drop their heads (sad) once they lose the ball, hang back (happy) once their team wins the ball, or freeze (panic) in transition rather than focus on the next task at hand. When these common psychological dynamics surface, encourage players to stay involved with the game's changes.

FITNESS

In a standard game, players require both physical and mental fitness so that the "head and body are closely linked" (Jankowski 2016, pg. 145). Maintaining a high level of game intensity will help players improve their ability to stay mentally alert over an extended period of physical exertion. Teams will need to overcome "tactical fatigue" in order to transition between multiple playing styles (Bordonau 2018, pg. 57).

Do not expect players to initially be able to maintain focus over long playing periods. When tactical fatigue is affecting team performance, evidenced by players making good decisions initially but poor ones as the game goes on, then the players should be provided more breaks during the game.

CHAPTER 3

COACHING: THE ART OF CHANGING BEHAVIOR

"The wall of frustration: (derives from) excessive importance of winning, excessive criticism, and lack of communication."

–From *The Principles of Brazilian Soccer* (Goncalves 1998, pg. 44)

"There should be no unnecessary yelling of instruction."

–Rinus Michels (Michels 2001, pg. 250)

Your mood and tone will directly influence how players react to your coaching instruction. It is important that you treat players well. The use of shame, guilt, anger, fear, and harsh physical punishments to motivate learning will decrease player motivation and contribute to player burnout if players take your tone personally and see themselves negatively. A player with a negative self-identity will have a lower tolerance for stress and thus be more easily overwhelmed by challenges. An encouraging, respectful coaching attitude is essential for players to develop self-efficacy, that is, confidence in themselves to overcome obstacles.

Good coaching is much more than setting up a drill for your players to do. However, even a perfect explanation and demonstration of a drill does not guarantee that players will learn how to do the skill or tactic well enough. Your coaching needs to change behaviors, and behaviors do not change easily. Your coaching should be deliberate and purposeful, attentive to every detail and focused on every mistake to assure the new behavior is correctly learned and remembered (Coyle 2009, pg. 51).

Coaching is two-fold. The coach's task is to stop bad habits and teach new behaviors, and this needs to be done decisively. Although learning and unlearning are separate processes, they go hand-in-hand, as one cannot be successful without the other. For example, if a player is trained to pass a ball perfectly, but there is no purposeful intervention to stop old ways of passing, the new learning may not be remembered. Under the pressure of a game a player is likely to return to old habits of passing.

The goal of coaching is to facilitate the right skills and tactics becoming deeply ingrained. However, reliance on verbal instruction alone is not enough to achieve this goal. You will need to use multiple coaching approaches. The right intervention at the right time can change the course of a season.

COACHING INTERVENTIONS

COACHING INTERVENTION: NEUROMUSCULAR TRAINING

"The great thing, then, in all education, is to make our nervous system our ally instead of our enemy."

–William James–"The father of American psychology" (James 1918, pg. 122)

"Strife inside the body equals strife with the ball."

–Marcel Lucassen (Honigstein 2015, pg.146)

"The goal is always the same: to break a skill into its component pieces."

(Coyle 2009, pg. 84)

Providing players with meaningful repetition is the most common approach to teaching skills and tactics. However, human behavior is resistant to change and prone to habits. Since correct soccer techniques and tactics can be counterintuitive, neuromuscular training should come before players practice skills with a ball. As described by neuroscientists, the general goal of neuromuscular training is to improve sensorimotor control and achieve compensatory functional stability.

In neuromuscular soccer skill training, each aspect of the soccer technique is broken down into specific body positions and simple movements in order to ensure the new skill is ingrained in the player's muscle memory. Neuromuscular training helps the player overcome the control and rigidity of the previous habits and correctly imprint the new behavior. Patiently insisting that a player hold the foot in a specific skill position can often improve player skill more than repeated verbal explanations and even demonstrations.

A player should be asked to do the skill with a ball only after the player can perfectly perform the skill positions and movements without the ball. The observant coach will notice that the specific problems not corrected in neuromuscular training will surface in the drills when the ball is introduced.

NEUROMUSCULAR TRAINING TEMPLATE

The coaching elements described in Chapter 5 conclude with specific neuromuscular training exercises. An advanced form of neuromuscular training to improve shooting can be found in the Appendix. There are four essential steps needed to complete the process for neuromuscular training of soccer skills.

1) SOCCER POSITION (ATHLETIC STANCE)

"Stand with your feet facing forward, knees softly bent, feet just wider than shoulder width, engaged at the core" (Fig. 3.1, *a* and *b*).

Fig. 3.1, a and b

Asking players to drop into this athletic stance position will help prepare them mentally and physically to do the neuromuscular training.

2) GROUNDED SKILL POSITION

"Place your feet in the correct position for the skill and hold that position with the playing foot still touching the ground."

Keeping the foot that will eventually strike the ball connected to the ground makes it easier for the players to hold the foot in the correct place. Connection with the ground is used to counter the pull of older, habitual body positions.

3) OPEN SKILL POSITION

"Lift the foot and hold it in the air in the correct skill position."

The first two steps are relatively easy, but this step can be much more difficult. Once the players lift one foot from the ground, then the body can struggle to hold the correct position for a couple of reasons:

- The foot will not want to stay in the right shape without the ground as an anchor, but revert to a more natural, straightened position.
- As the foot lifts, the body also wants to lift, since the player will instinctively want the distance between the foot and the body to remain the same.

You might need to correct both problems before moving on to the next step. Not correcting the issues will likely lead to the players having difficulty performing the skill with the ball later in the practice session. Here are interventions to help correct the problems players might have with the open skill position:

- Have players place the foot back on the ground to regain the correct foot position before lifting the foot again. Give the players time to figure out how to engage the right muscle groups to balance on one foot in this awkward position. Model the correct body position for them yourself or have an advanced player do it.
- As the foot lifts, tell the players to "crunch" the center of their bodies like an accordion by tightening their stomach muscles. They should also bend their knees to counter the tendency to stretch upward as the foot lifts in the air. The distance between the foot and torso should be smaller than it was when the foot was on the ground.

In the open skill position the foot will sometimes shake as the player struggles to keep it in the right skill position without the ground as an anchor. Once players can show they are stable and poised in the "foot-off-the-ground" position, then the players are ready to move to the next step. You should remain calm and patient during this learning process since it is essential for "perfect" skill acquisition that players learn to do the open skill position correctly.

Once players can hold the open skill position, you should tell them to visualize doing the skill with an imaginary ball. Visualizing performing the skill will increase the player's ability to do the actual skill in practice.

4) SKILL

"Perform the skill."

After learning the body positions and movements of the skill, players are asked to perform the skill with a stationary ball. Next, players perform the skill while dribbling or moving around the area. Finally, players can accelerate after doing the skill.

COACHING INTERVENTION: FREEZING

During soccer drills, a common intervention is to stop the practice, discuss the problem, demonstrate the solution, and have the players rehearse the correction before resuming playing. This multi-step process can take precious minutes from a practice, but can be very effective at improving player techniques and tactics.

Freezing the drill not only provides an opportunity to teach a new skill but perhaps even more important, can stop a bad habit. Players want to play, and when a competitive game is stopped in the midst of the action, players get annoyed and detest the break—which they experience as a negative consequence. Players will then try not to make the same mistake, not just because of the coach's teaching during the freeze, but also because they want to keep playing.

Letting players play is the best reward. Freezing a positive moment can inadvertently lead to the extinguishing of a positive behavior that the coach wants to reinforce. It would be better to talk about a positive play at a natural break, or just praise players during the run of play.

COACHING INTERVENTION: COACHING DURING THE GAME

Coaches often instruct players during a drill or game. The timing of the coaching intervention should be clearly linked to what is happening on the field so that the player has little choice but to listen and obey the directive. If you speak too soon or too late, then the coaching intervention will not be nearly as impactful.

You should be very specific about what you are trying to improve, rather than directing every play. For example, in a drill working on build up under moderate pressure, the goal is for midfielders to check to the ball and do half-turns across the body that will protect the ball. If players continue to turn into the opponent and lose the ball, you can intervene by directing them to "turn across your body" right before they receive the ball. Once they accomplish the turn, then there is no more for you to say.

Coaching within the game can help players overcome entrenched habits. Non-specific continuous coaching, i.e., joy-sticking, should be avoided. You want to train your players to listen for your instructions. Joy-sticking will lead your players to either ignore your instructions altogether or become dependent on your advice, which can encourage players to second-guess their instincts.

COACHING INTERVENTION: DRILL CHANGE

It can be difficult to know exactly how players will respond to a drill prior to a practice. Change the field size, player numbers, and rules of a game to improve player learning. Players can benefit from cones placed in the field that mark where players should run. Drill alterations are important to ensure that players are appropriately challenged.

COACHING INTERVENTION: CONSEQUENCES

"The consequences of an act affect the probability of it occurring again."
—*Attributed to* B.F. Skinner—behavioral psychologist

"Hiddink accepts technical and tactical mistakes. But he does not tolerate mental weaknesses because they threaten the team effort."
(Meijer 2006, pg. 103)

Players have been given physical exercises ("consequences")—for example, push-ups, sprints, knee jumps, etc.—to get them to stop stubborn habits. *Consequences should only be applied as a last resort.* Before that, you will use neuromuscular training, explanations, demonstrations, rehearsals, coaching within the game, and drill changes to improve player learning.

Consequences should not be imposed when a player makes a mistake with skills, for example, with a bad pass or a poor shot. Players who are slow to improve their technique should be asked to do simpler drills or repeat aspects of neuromuscular training until the skills improve. Punishing a poor technique will often discourage players from taking chances on performing that technique in future practices and games. For example, punishing a player who misses a shot on goal will likely result in the player becoming less inclined to shoot, rather than eager to perfect shooting technique.

The best use of consequences is when the culprit is not poor skills but mental laziness. If, after you have used other more benign interventions, players still struggle to "remember," punishing them with a push-up at the moment they make an error may improve their decision-making. Waiting for the end of practice is not as effective in changing behaviors because the response is too distant from the mistake. If the problem is particularly stubborn, then the player can do progressively more push-ups each time the same "lazy" mistake is made: one push-up for the first mistake, two push-ups for the second, and so on.

BALANCED COACHING

Practices are organized so that drills that require intensive learning of new skills and tactics alternate with competitive games where the new ideas are integrated and consolidated. Here are recommended interventions for your practices that will balance learning with playing:

- The warm-up game should be uninterrupted so that players can demonstrate that they are consolidating previous learning. You should direct players at opportune moments during the run of play and offer explanations and brief demonstrations during natural stoppages.

- With a focus on perfecting new skills and tactics, Stage 1 drills require frequent drill interruptions, rehearsals, explanations, demonstrations, drill changes and neuromuscular training. It is imperative that you intervene as much as necessary for players to learn the new skills and tactics correctly, otherwise, ensuing drills with added pressure will be much less effective.

- The small-sided games in Stage 2 should be uninterrupted as players practice the new teaching in competitive play. When necessary, direct players during the run of play to promote learning. Provide feedback and briefly demonstrate corrections between games while players recover.

- To learn how to apply the new skills and tactics playing within a formation on a standard field, players will again need intrusive coaching interventions during the Stage 3 positional games. Freezing the game at important moments in order to rehearse corrections will help players integrate the new ideas. You have an opportunity to provide explanations and further demonstrations between plays, since the positional games can entail frequent restarts. Alter the drill to ensure correct learning and player success.

- The standard game, at the end of practice, should not be interrupted very frequently. Offer directives and explanations during the run of play and brief demonstrations at the break. Freeze the game one (or two) occasions to support the team's incorporating the learning from the practice with lessons from previous trainings.

CHAPTER 4

INTRODUCTION TO THE PRACTICE DIAGRAMS

GLOSSARY OF PRACTICE DIAGRAM SYMBOLS

In the practice diagrams, the red players typically denote the players who are the focus of the exercise and the white players are their opponents. Players in yellow represent bumpers (Fig. 4.1).

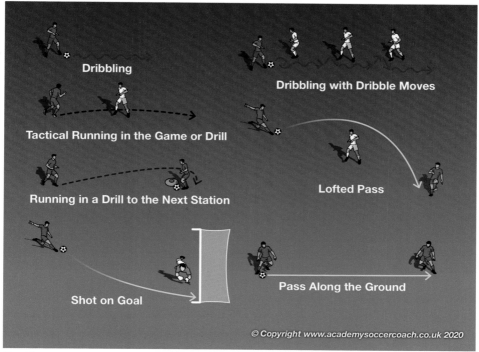

Fig. 4.1

THE 4-3-3 FORMATION (11V11)

The practice plans are based around your team playing a 4-3-3, which signifies that your team will play four players in the defense, three in the midfield, and three in attack. The goalkeeper is assumed to be on the field and thus is not generally mentioned in the line-up configuration—otherwise it would be called a 1-4-3-3, since you start the numbering from the defense moving toward the forwards.

The 4-3-3 is adaptive to a variety of playing styles. As shown in Fig. 4.2, your team will have dominant numbers in the center of the field with the three midfielders (A), access to the important wide, forward areas with the wing forwards (B), and ample coverage in defense and support with build up with the four defenders (D). The center forward also provides an important target (C). Three forwards also allow your team to effectively press the opponent's backline. The defenders and the attackers are typically spread out across the field in a line, but the three midfielders can be placed in a number of different ways:

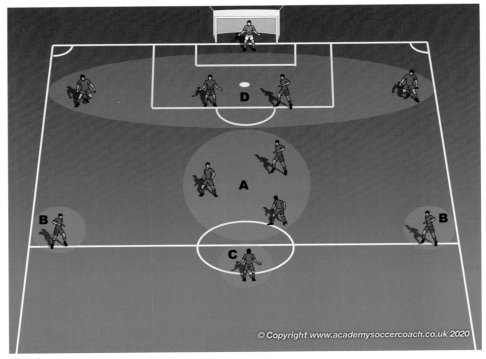

Fig. 4.2

- The three central midfielders in an off-set triangle, a dynamic formation (Fig. 4.2).
- The three central midfielders placed in a 2-1, a defensive formation (Fig. 4.3).

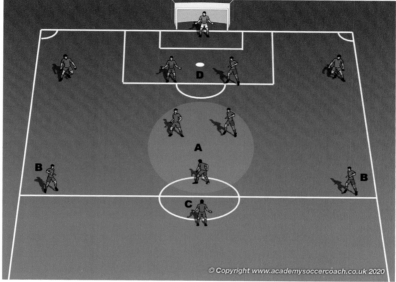

Fig. 4.3

- The three central midfielders placed in a 1-2, an attacking formation (Fig. 4.4).

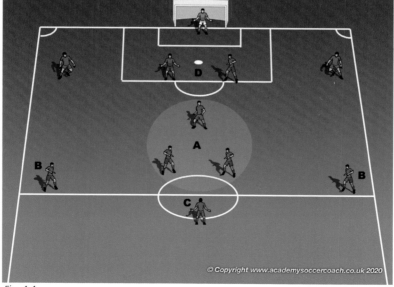

Fig. 4.4

The starting position for a team dictates the primary areas of the field that players will defend and attack. However, the positioning of players will change during the game, depending on whether the team is attacking or defending and on the location of the ball and opponents.

Following are examples of how the 4-3-3 formation can provide flexibility in how your team can attack and defend:

- An outside back can move upfield and play as a forward to create a 3-3-4 formation in order to increase the number of attacking players (Fig. 4.5).

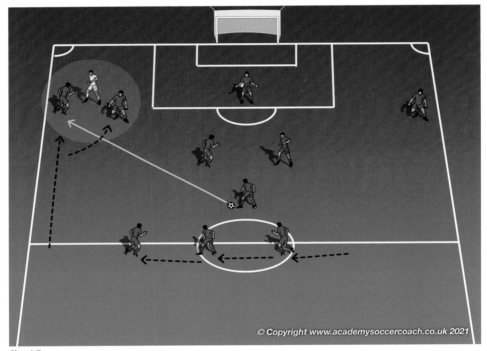

Fig. 4.5

- Both outside backs can step up into the midfield to create a 2-5-3 formation (Fig. 4.6).

Fig. 4.6

- A central midfielder can move forward to provide support for the center forward, creating a 4-2-4 formation (Fig. 4.7). The left and right wing forwards can also add support to the center forward.

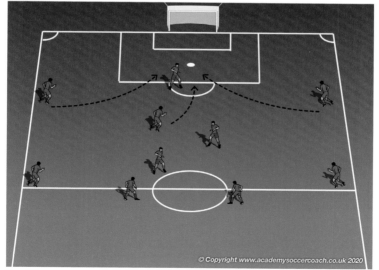

Fig. 4.7

- A wing forward can drop back into the midfield to create a 4-4-2 formation (Fig. 4.8).

Fig. 4.8

If you or your club is committed to playing the recommended 4-3-3 formation, then use formations with reduced numbers in practice or games to prepare the team. These formations should emphasize solid defending, a dynamic midfield, and width in attack. Here are examples of formations that could be used:

6V6 FORMATION—2-2-1 (2-3)

In attack, the outside midfielders push forward to provide width, and one of the center backs steps forward to provide central support in the midfield. In defense, an outside midfielder can drop back into the defensive line (Fig. 4.9).

Fig. 4.9

7V7 FORMATION—2-3-1

In attack, the two outside midfielders push forward to provide width, and a center back steps forward to provide extra support in the midfield. When defending, outside midfielders can drop back to provide extra support in defense, so you defend with a back line of three defenders (Fig. 4.10).

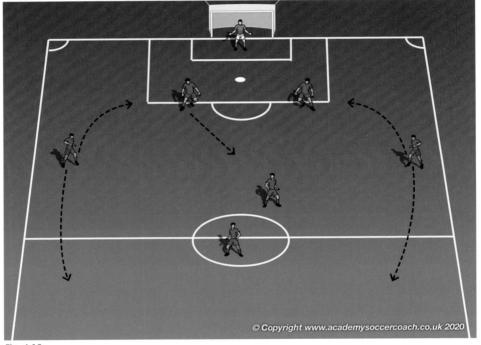

Fig. 4.10

8V8 FORMATION—2-4-1

The two players in the center of the field afford dynamic midfield play. In attack, the outside midfielders go forward. The defensive center midfielder can drop back into the defensive line to ensure the team is always defending with at least three players. This formation is much more flexible but riskier than the 3-3-1 formation, which starts off with three set defenders. In a 3-3-1, the center back would step up into the midfield to support the attack and the outside midfielders would again push forward. The 3-3-1 is more stable defensively, but less dynamic in the midfield (Fig. 4.11).

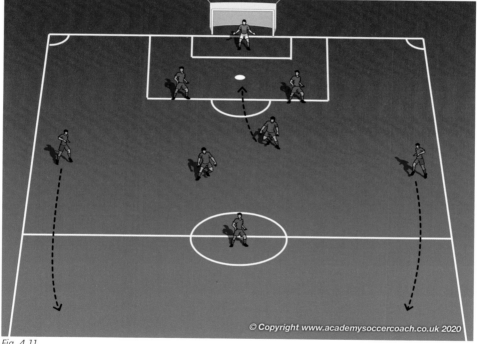

Fig. 4.11

9V9 FORMATION—3-2-3

In attack, you begin with two wing forwards, a central striker, and two central midfield players (one more attacking and one more defensive), with a solid line of three defenders in the back. In attack, one outside back can push forward and add support in the midfield. In defense, a wing forward will drop back into the midfield to create a line of three (Fig. 4.12).

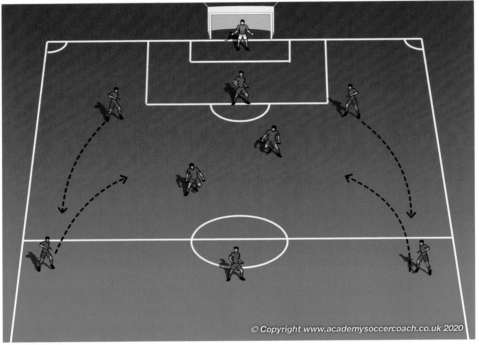

Fig. 4.12

PLAYER POSITIONAL IDENTIFICATION

Although soccer coaches can use numbers to describe a player's positioning (Fig. 4.13), you might find it easier to communicate with your players about positions using the names and abbreviations of each position (Fig. 4.14).

- Goalkeeper (GK)
- Right Fullback (RB)
- Right Center Back (RCB)
- Left Center Back (LCB)
- Left Fullback (LB)
- Center Defensive Midfielder (DM)
- Center Midfielder (CM)
- Attacking Midfielder (AM)
- Left Wing Forward (LW)
- Center Forward (CF)
- Right Wing Forward (RW)

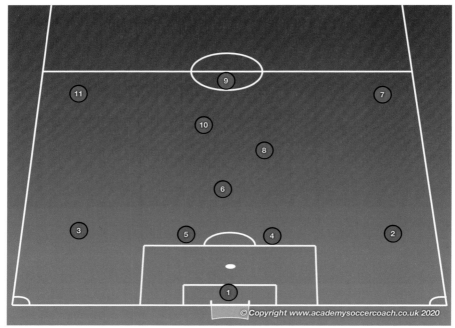

Fig. 4.13

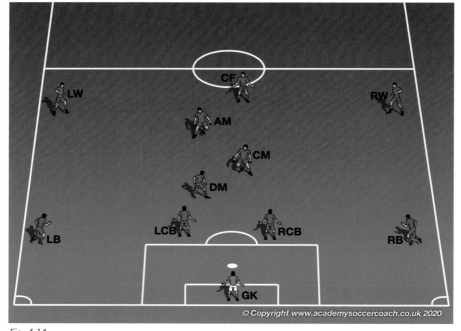

Fig. 4.14

THE POSITIONING OF THE COACH DURING A PRACTICE EXERCISE

You should be positioned in a way to have the best impact on the drill, depending on what you want to emphasize. In a common exercise where the attacking team plays to an end zone against a defense, you could stand in a number of areas to impact the play of the game. For example, as seen in Fig. 4.15, standing behind the attackers (A) allows you to best instruct the three midfielders. Standing behind the defense allows you to better coach the forwards and the defenders (B). Standing on one side of the field or the other allows you to focus your coaching on the play in wide areas (C). In this last scenario, you will need to switch sides or switch players halfway through the drill to ensure balanced coaching in these areas.

Although you should typically stand outside the field of play, in order to stay out of the way of the players doing the drill, there are times when you should consider standing in the center of the exercise area. From the center of the field, you can more easily offer directions to individual players without always having to stop play, especially when the exercise area is rather large.

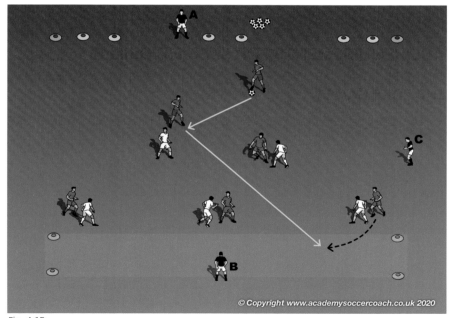

Fig. 4.15

THE SPACE REQUIREMENTS FOR EACH EXERCISE

An essential art of coaching is knowing how large an area to use when marking out a field for a drill. The drill can be made easier or harder by increasing or decreasing the size of the playing area. The shape of the space—say, a square versus a rectangle or a circle versus a square—can also impact player learning.

The exact space requirement for each drill is not listed for every exercise, since the space required can vary greatly depending on your players' skill level, athleticism, and age. The space provided to your team to train will dictate the size of space you will use, since many coaches don't have access to a whole field or even a half-field for every practice.

When possible, teams should do drills in the areas of the field where the actual skills and tactics will be used in standard games. For example, the probing drills should be done between the penalty box and the halfway line with players positioned and facing the way they would in the game. Positioning players in the correct places on the field for a drill will provide the drill with more of a standard game-like feeling, which in turn will help players express the learned skills and tactics in a game.

SPACE REQUIREMENTS FOR SPECIFIC DRILLS

A) END ZONE GAMES

End zone games are often used in Stage 3 positional games when the offense plays against the defense. In end zone games, one or both teams score by passing to a teammate or dribbling into an area called the end zone, located at the end of the field. A field with an end zone should be wide enough so that the back line of defenders cannot easily cover the whole distance.

B) POSSESSION GAMES

In a possession game with the goal of teaching players how to pass safely away from pressure, a rectangular field offers players width to pass to an open area. The field, in general, should be large enough so that the receiving player has time on the ball to trap, look up, and pick out a player who will also have the time to pass the ball. However, expanding the playing area can also make the drill more difficult, since younger and inexperienced players will be challenged to make longer passes.

Adding or subtracting defenders will contribute to the challenges of keeping possession by increasing or reducing pressure on the ball. Also, the speed and strength of the defenders is an important variable when deciding on the size of the playing area and the number of defenders—especially at the youth level, where overall athletic ability can vary greatly.

C) 1V1 DRIBBLING GAMES

The key variable in a dribbling game is the width of the field. The field should be wide enough for players to have a realistic chance at dribbling past an opponent, which typically takes a dribbler at an angle away from the defender. A field that is too narrow could result in player frustration and less learning. Coaches should monitor the success of dribblers and widen or narrow the field to make the drill easier or harder.

COMPETITIVE GAME RULES

A) SCORING

Competitive games are directly influenced by the scoring system. You need to imagine how your players will react to your scoring system based on their ability level and the learning objectives of the practice. The reward for trying new skills must be greater than the risk of making mistakes. Give harder skills and tactics more points when players need incentives to do certain activities within a game. You can use multiple scoring systems in a single game: Teams can score one point for a goal, two points for completing a wall pass, and three points to dribble around an opponent using a specified move. Also, the point system should be the same level of difficulty for each team, even when they have different ways to score. Adjust the scoring system within the game to ensure competitiveness and learning.

Giving points for consecutive passes is a general scoring rule in competitive games where the goal is to improve a team's ability to keep possession of the ball. However, in drills where players can score by dribbling or wall passing past a defender, adding a consecutive passing rule forces the defending team to apply pressure to the ball. Players are savvy about winning, and if they know that a wall pass is worth extra points, they might run away from the situations where a wall pass could be made around them.

B) TOUCH LIMITATION RULES

Coaches restrict the number of touches players use with each play to speed up passing and improve possession. Limiting how many touches your players can use per play can sometimes decrease possession and reduce a team's chances of speeding up play.

In a typical game situation, the players with the ball will often be pressured by the opposition from the front, making it difficult to "pass the way they face" even when done quickly with one or two touches. A key to keeping possession is for players to turn away from the opponent, which is not always possible to do with one or two touches. In many circumstances, trapping, turning, and passing will take a minimum of three to four touches, since after the turn a player will take a quick preparatory touch to ensure the ball is perfectly lined up to pass.

Even when the objective of the drill is to improve the speed of play, forcing players to only play one touch may increase the number of times the attacking team will lose the ball, reducing opportunities to practice quick passing sequences. Also, requiring that players do one or two touches can reinforce the wrong habits, like rushing a pass, always passing forward (or backward), and attempting to pass the ball through the opponent—what I describe as "forcing through ankles."

"Bumpers," who provide extra support for the team in possession, are an exception, and they should have touch limitations. Bumpers are typically not put under pressure, so without some touch or time limitation the game can bog down as bumpers sit on the ball without any incentive to play more quickly.

INTERVENTIONS TO INCREASE SPEED OF PLAY WITHOUT RESTRICTING PLAYER TOUCHES

- Tell your players that they need to increase the tempo of play during the drill and praise quick passing sequences.
- Include a rule that three to five one-touch passes in a row score a point (or more).
- Add bumpers to the game so players have more passing opportunities.

INTERVENTIONS TO IMPROVE POSSESSION WITHOUT RESTRICTING PLAYER TOUCHES

- Encourage players within a drill to turn away from pressure and not "force through ankles."
- Provide a big enough playing area for players to trap and pass the ball without too much pressure from the defenders.
- Improve player passing and trapping skills before the possession game to ensure players have sufficient skills to do the drill.

BUMPERS V NEUTRALS

At times, the practice plans in the next chapter will include the use of bumpers, who are players standing on the edge of the playing area and passing to one or both teams after the ball is passed to them. Bumpers typically are not allowed to enter the field of play but only provide support for the players on the field to help ensure the team in possession has more players than the defending team. The extra support of bumpers can help teams learn difficult lessons, such as keeping possession or creating wall passes. Once teams can successfully perform the necessary skills and tactics with bumpers, then the bumpers are reduced in number before being removed altogether.

"Neutrals," on the other hand, is a term used here to describe players who play within the game and switch teams depending on which team has possession of the ball. For example, in a 5v5 game, an eleventh player with a different color jersey would join the team that possesses the ball to make the game a 6v5 advantage for the attacking team. Neutrals can confuse other players since they are engaged in moment-to-moment play while rapidly switching teams depending on who has the ball.

HOW TO AVOID THE USE OF NEUTRAL PLAYERS

- Substitute players into the game rather than confuse the game by adding a neutral player.
- Play one team with fewer—but better or more athletic players—against a team with more players to ensure competitiveness.
- Change the scoring rules to ensure appropriate competitiveness between teams.
- Use bumpers to give the team in possession extra support.

EQUIPMENT

A) CONES

Use low-profile disc cones—about 2 inches tall by 8 inches in diameter—in your drills rather than the taller, pointier "traffic" cones, sometimes referred to as "marker" cones. The disc cones do not tip over as easily as the traffic cones. Even when they do get knocked around, they tend to stay in the appropriate position and continue to work as a functional indicator of a specific spot. Though more traditional and more visible, traffic cones are easily knocked over and can even roll away, which can cause confusion about the boundaries of an exercise. Reserve traffic cones for indicating the halfway line, offsides line, and other important areas of a field where they are not directly involved in the field of play. When cones have different purposes, but are near each other, use disc cones of different colors. Also, when using traffic cones, make sure to purchase cones with slits that collapse upon impact, rather than the solid cones that could injure a player who falls on one.

Besides many disc cones and a few traffic cones, it will be important to have a handful of flat poly spot markers. These poly spot markers are typically used on wooden gym floors where they don't slide around like plastic disc cones. Poly spot markers are useful for drills in which players are required to step on the cones to play the game. The use of poly spot markers can be essential when setting up passing patterns, since inexperienced players will often wait for the next pass behind the cone (despite instruction not to), making it very difficult for them to trap a ball that comes careening unpredictably off the disc cone in front of them. However, because disc cones are more challenging to dribble around, they are still ideal for dribbling drills when the player has full control of the ball. Some players will take advantage of the flat poly spot marker cones and dribble over them.

B) SOCCER BALLS

You usually can't go wrong buying an expensive soccer ball or two for actual games, but picking out the ideal and affordable practice soccer ball can be challenging. Practice balls can vary in quality—not always related to the price of the ball. Before investing in precious resources, order a selection of practice soccer balls and test them out. Sometimes the actual quality of a ball will not be known until after it has been kicked around for a couple of weeks. Some soccer balls will last three or more seasons, while others will begin to show wear and tear after only a couple of practices.

The weight and texture of the ball can affect player skill development. Hard plastic soccer balls can hurt young feet, whereas soccer balls that are too spongy can make it difficult for players to fine-tune their skill development. A practice ball should also be water-repellent, whereas a game ball does not need to be since it can dry out for a week before being used again.

I prefer lighter-weight size 5 soccer balls, which are more fun to play with, do not hurt as much when heading, and ensure that players develop a softer touch on the ball. However, younger players using a size 3 or 4 soccer ball are okay using a thicker-skinned, durable soccer ball since they are using the ball mostly on the ground and can benefit from a ball that does not fly away at every touch.

Also, before every practice make sure your soccer balls are properly inflated. Do not necessarily rely on the guidelines on the ball, as the pressure indicated as ideal for the ball can sometimes make the ball too firm and thus more difficult and uncomfortable to use. A stand-up bicycle pump works well to quickly inflate a bag of soccer balls. One way to tell if a ball is properly inflated is to press down on the ball with the palm of your hand to see if it gives a bit under a moderate amount of pressure. If the ball does not give under a moderate amount of pressure, then it is too hard; if your palm sinks some into the ball, then it is too soft.

COACHING POSITIONAL SOCCER

C) GOALS

Soccer goals are expensive. You can save money by buying two lightweight, portable, fold-up goals that can be placed together to form the width of a standard goal, although not generally the standard height. Kickbacks, where the net drops straight down, are often better than a goal for practices because the ball will bounce back to players. Even for young players, buy a regular 24-x-8-foot kickback, and place cones in front of it to designate the goal. The large kickback will save players time retrieving the ball when they miss, which will provide them with more shooting opportunities. A smaller goal will not necessarily improve a player's aim. With a smaller target, players may shoot with restraint because they are afraid of missing the goal and having to make a long run to retrieve the ball.

If you are practicing on a field with standard goals, then it can be much easier to set up the portable goals or kickback at the right distance to make your field smaller. Moving large goals is especially difficult, and even dangerous, if the goals are heavy, broken, and half-buried in the ground.

Remember that all goals need to be anchored properly to the ground. The best way to anchor goals is to put weighted bags of sand on the goals' nets and side/back bars. Metal stakes can easily come out. Weighted bags of sand can be made by doubling up black construction bags and filling them with playground sand. More durable canvas bags with handles can be purchased from soccer companies; 70-pound sandbags can be found at hardware stores, but they should be reduced in weight if you need to regularly transport them from field to field.

CHAPTER 5

THE ELEVEN
COACHING ELEMENTS

COACHING ELEMENT #1
PASSING AROUND LIGHT PRESSURE

Philipp Lahm of FC Bayern Munich passes out of the defense.

Phase of Play	Build-Up
Coaching Element	#1 Passing Around Light Pressure
Development Stage	I Skills and Tactics
Drill	"Passing Around the Square"

Learning Objective

Players will learn how to trap the ball across the body and accurately pass the ball.

Drill Description

Players pass the ball around the square. Players follow their passes to the next cone. Before players receive a pass, they must move away from the cone, i.e., drop back from the cone when they receive a pass in order to create the right angle and space to pass to the next player (Fig. 5.1a).

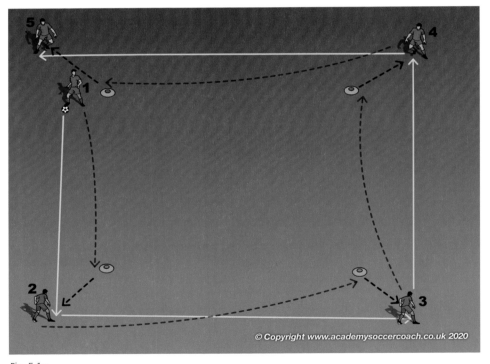

Fig. 5.1a

Player Principles

1.1 Players need to be in a "supportive position" to receive the pass.

Player 2 will drop back from the cone at the correct angle to trap and pass the ball to the next player (5.1*a*). If the receiving player checks too close to the passer, then the receiver will not be able to change the direction of play with two touches (Fig. 5.1*b*).

Fig. 5.1b

1.2 Players should "receive the ball with the second (outside) foot."

The second or outside foot is the foot farthest away from the player who made the pass. As you can see in figure 5.1*a*, player 1 passes to player 2, who made space to receive the ball by checking back. Player 2 traps the ball with the inside of the second foot, which allows player 2 to pass the ball to player 3.

1.3 Players need to "communicate" that they are open.

As the ball is moving toward player 2, player 3 needs to communicate being open to receiving a pass from player 2. This timely communication will cue player 2 to trap the ball with the second or outside foot in order to switch the direction of the play (Fig. 5.1a).

Skills Introduced
Trapping

- Receive with the inside of the second (outside) foot in order to switch the field
- Receive with the outside of the foot in order to switch the field

Passing

- Push pass
- Squib pass, i.e., a long skimming pass with the instep

Dribbling

- Roll back

Tactics

- The receiver drops back to receive the pass to create the best angle of support for trapping the ball with the second foot and quickly switching the direction of play
- Players communicate in a timely manner about being open for a pass

Drill Progression

1. Beginner players pass on the inside of the square to focus on the trapping and passing techniques (Fig. 5.2).

2. Players pass the ball around the outside of the cones. Players will drop back into the correct supportive position to receive a pass. Pass counterclockwise around the square so players can trap and pass with the inside of the right foot (Fig. 5.1a).

3. Players pass clockwise around the square using their left foot to trap the ball, but still passing with the inside of the right foot.

4. Players pass clockwise around the cones and trap the ball with the outside of the right foot and then pass with the inside of the right foot.

5. Players receive with the inside of the left foot and pass with the inside of the left foot.

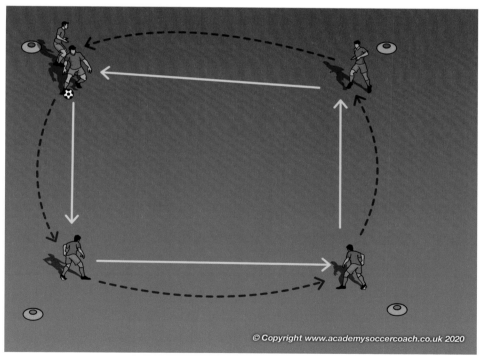

Fig. 5.2

6.   Players receive the ball, dribble forward a couple of yards before turning, dribbling back toward the original spot and passing back in the same direction from which they received the pass. In this drill, players do not follow the pass (Fig. 5.3). This drill focuses on the important skill of turning away from pressure. (This drill can directly follow passing around the square using the same square configuration, though it is best if there are at least two players on each cone.)

Fig. 5.3

Drill Variations

- Add a second ball. The initial pass must start at a cone with two players. (You will need at least six players per square to use two soccer balls.)
- Increase the speed of passing and trapping.
- Players change passing directions when you yell, "Switch!"
- Make the trap more positive, i.e., a longer touch toward the receiver to increase the speed of play and allow the passer to get to a sprint faster after making the pass.
- Make a rectangle with cones so players have to pass longer distances on two sides.
- Players must dribble halfway to the next cone before passing.
- Place one passing square inside another passing square to save space and provide passing opportunities at different distances (Fig. 5.4). This arrangement also helps raise the intensity of the drill since players are so close together.
- Add indirect pressure by overlapping passing squares or rectangles (Fig. 5.5, *a* and *b*).

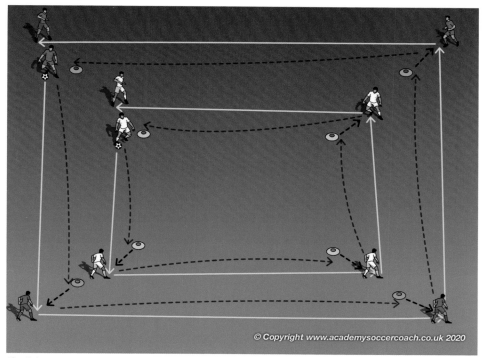

Fig. 5.4

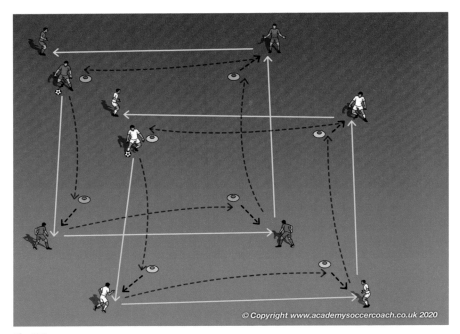

Fig. 5.5a

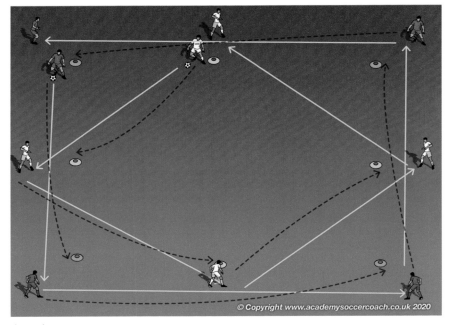

Fig. 5.5b

Coaching Interventions

Problem #1

The passer is unable to pass the ball straight and on the ground to the receiver.

Possible Cause: The passer does not directly face the receiver when making the pass and thus is not be able to strike the ball correctly with the inside of the foot.

Practice Intervention: *Freeze—Demonstrate how to face the receiver when passing the ball. Explain that even facing at a slight angle away from the receiver will make it much more difficult to pass the ball straight and on the ground. Rehearse the proper passing form.

Problem #2

The player is not able to receive and pass the ball to the next player with two touches.

Possible Cause #1: The receiver traps the ball at the wrong angle to make the next pass.

Practice Intervention: *Freeze—If the receiver is too close to the cone or has checked too close to the passer then there will not be enough space to trap the ball across the body as shown in Fig. 5.1b. Demonstrate the type of angle required to receive the ball and switch directions. *Drill Change—You can also place a poly spot marker where you want the players to drop back to receive the pass to ensure they create the correct passing angle.

Possible Cause #2: The receiver has poor trapping technique. The ball bounces away from the receiver or the ball is too close to the player to make a pass without touching the ball a second time.

Practice Intervention: *Freeze—Show how to trap the ball across the body in the new direction. This trap involves a small hop on the planting foot as the ball is received in order to change the angle of the body and pass in a new direction. *Neuromuscular training—Practice the correct body positions to correctly trap the ball (same as the push-pass).

Possible Cause #3: The pass is too soft or too hard to trap properly.

Practice Intervention: *Freeze—Demonstrate the proper weight of a pass that is ideal for the receiver to make the trap. Players should rehearse passing correctly.

Possible Cause #4: Players are flat-footed and do not adjust quickly enough to the pass.

Practice Intervention: *Freeze—A player who does not move quickly enough from side to side to position the trapping foot correctly will have a more difficult time switching directions with the trap. You should show players how to stay active on the balls of their feet so they can quickly adjust side to side to receiving the ball with the second foot. Even if the pass is not played directly to the second foot, the receiver should shuffle quickly to the side to trap the ball correctly. *Direct—During the run of play, you can offer timely suggestions to the receiver when to quickly move to the side to trap the pass with the second foot.

Competitive Game

Passing Around the Square Competition—Easy Drill
Groups compete with one another to see who can pass around the square five times the fastest. If a team makes a mistake, then the whole team has to do a push-up before continuing.

Variation: This competition can be made more challenging and more fun when the passing boxes overlap (see Fig. 5.5, *a* and *b*).

Other Exercises

Positional Exercise: "Build-Up Possession Shadow Play"—Moderate Difficulty
Four fullbacks pass to each other in passing patterns (Fig. 5.6, *a* and *b*). Players need to shift their positions to ensure the proper angles of support. All the same passing, trapping and communication lessons learned above apply to this drill. Initially, players pass the ball from side to side. Next, players move the ball upfield with instructions for what to do on the way to the halfway line: 1) make 10 passes, 2) switch the ball from one side of the field to the other 3 times, 3) complete 4 turns, i.e., roll backs, or 4) any combination of passing and turning. The squib pass is used for long passes.

Drill Variation: Add two opponents who provide moderate pressure on the ball.

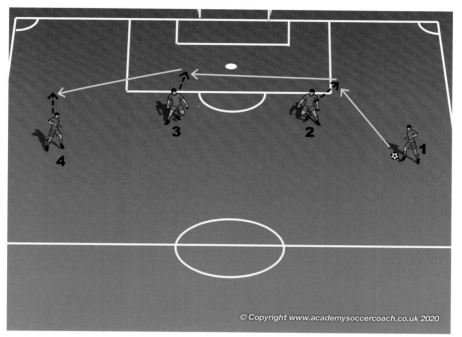

Fig. 5.6a

Fig. 5.6b

Two-Player Trapping Drill—Easy Drill

Player 1 passes to player 2 who traps the ball across the body and dribbles past the farthest cone, stops the ball and passes to player 1. Player 1 traps the ball across the body and dribbles back past the starting cone before passing back to player 2. Change directions to use the other foot (Fig. 5.7).

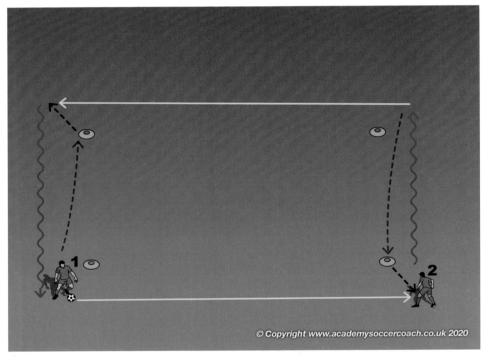

Fig. 5.7

One-Player Trapping Drill—Easy Drill

The player passes off the wall and traps the ball behind the cone with the second foot, then dribbles to the opposite side and repeats the drill (Fig. 5.8).

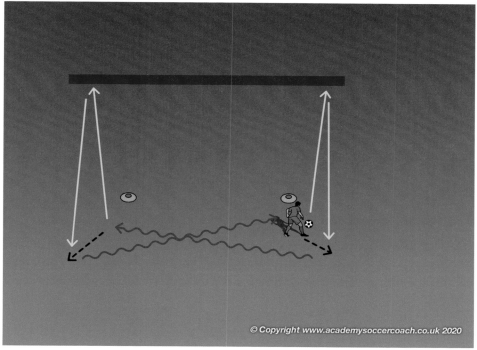

Fig. 5.8

Phase of Play	Build-Up
Coaching Element	#1 Passing Around Light Pressure
Development Stage	II Competitive Game
Drill	"4v2 Light Pressure Possession Game"

Learning Objective

Players will learn how to keep possession under light pressure.

Drill Description

4v2

Four players inside a rectangular area keep possession against two players. A diamond set out in the middle of the playing area with poly spot markers delineates the defender's restricted zone. Only one defender can leave the restricted zone at a time to try to win the ball. The four players score by making four to seven consecutive passes, and the two players in the middle score by winning the ball and dribbling out of the rectangle (Fig. 5.9).

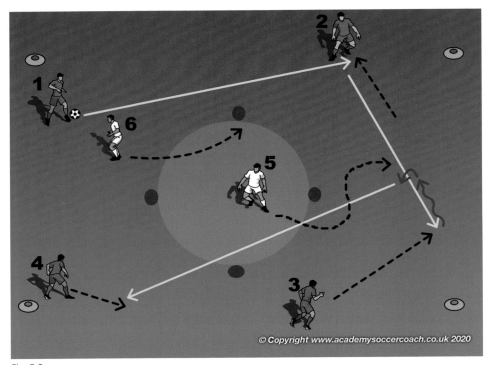

Fig. 5.9

Player Principles

1.4 Players "trap away from pressure."

Example: Player 1 plays to player 2 who receives the ball across the body with the second (left) foot. This allows player 2 to open up to the whole field and look for the best passing option, such as passing to player 3. Since the player who passes the ball is typically under pressure (player 6 challenging player 1), the receiver (player 2) is usually better off trapping the ball away from the direction of the passer, rather than back toward the passer.

1.5 Players "drop off to support the passer" with deep angles.

Example: Player 3 moves into a better position to support player 2 even before player 2 receives the ball. Player 3 will communicate with player 2 about being open to receive a pass.

1.6 Players should "turn away from pressure" and not force passes through defenders.

Example: Player 3 receives the ball and is shut down by defending player 5. Player 3 turns away from pressure and does not try to play through the defender.

Drill Progression

1. Play 4v1 without the restricted zone for the defender.
2. Play 4v2 (see Fig. 5.9), as described previously. Note: Defenders should communicate with one another about who is pressing and who is staying in the zone.
3. Enlarge the playing area so passes have to be longer and more accurate. (This can make the game harder for beginner players, but potentially easier for better players who already can pass longer distances.)
4. Enlarge the restricted zone so defenders can put more pressure on the ball.

Drill Variation

- Play 6v3 in a larger area—two defenders can leave the restricted zone at one time (Fig. 5.10).

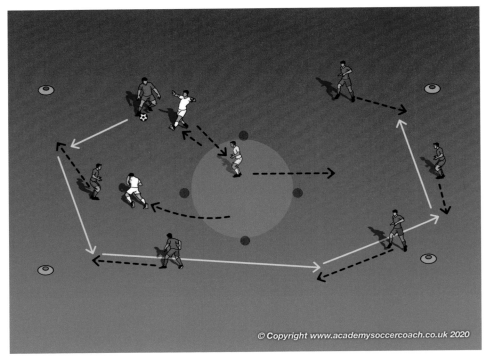

Fig. 5.10

Coaching Interventions

Problem #1

Passes are intercepted by the defenders.

Possible Cause #1: The player is passing toward defensive pressure.

Practice Intervention: *Demonstrate—Between games, demonstrate how to switch sides by trapping with the second foot or use a turn to avoid defensive pressure. Explain how trapping toward the passer will often take the player into pressure. Stress that the receiver of a pass should have some idea where to pass before receiving the ball. *Direct—At the right moment during the run of play, encourage the player to trap or turn away from trouble.

Possible Cause #2: The passer has no support.

Practice Intervention: *Demonstrate—Between games, show players how to anticipate and move into a supportive position while the ball is in transit to the next player. Explain that they cannot receive a pass unless they have a "clear view of the ball," i.e., no opponents between them and the ball. *Direct—When the ball is passed, remind the supporting players that, "Ball moves, we move." They must move into a correct supportive position before the receiver traps the ball and looks up to make the next pass. Tell supporting players to communicate to the passer when they are open to receive a pass.

Other Exercise

6v3 Passing Around Light Pressure Positional Game—Advanced Drill
Five field players and a goalkeeper keep possession away from three opponents in a third of the field. The six players score a point by making ten consecutive passes. The three opponents score on the goal for a point after winning the ball. The opponents are allowed to have two players at a time leave the restricted zone (Fig. 5.11).

Fig. 5.11

Phase of Play	Build-Up
Coaching Element	#1 Passing Around Light Pressure
Development Stage	III Positional Game
Drill	"5v2 Build-Up Under Light Pressure Over the Halfway Line"

Learning Objective

Players will learn how to advance the ball forward under light pressure from an opponent.

Drill Description

5v2

The four defenders and the goalkeeper attempt to move the ball over the halfway line without losing it and giving the forwards an easy chance to score on goal. The defenders must dribble over the halfway line to receive a point. The forwards score on goal for a point (Fig. 5.12).

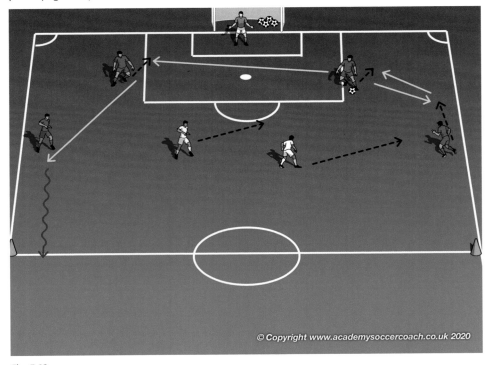

Fig. 5.12

Player Principles

1.7 "Safety v Risk:" Make the correct decision about when to go forward and when to pass backward.

The goal of build-up is to move the ball toward the opponent's goal. Players in possession of the ball need to assess whether they can advance or should pass backward.

1.8 "No square passes:" Receiving players should offer angled support behind the player on the ball instead of providing support straight across or level with the passer.

Players off the ball need to find the correct angles to support the player on the ball. In possession build up under light pressure, supportive players need to drop back with deep enough angles to the ball to ensure the passer can make a safe pass. A pass made straight across the field, called a "square pass," is riskier because when an opponent intercepts the ball there is potentially little support to win it back.

Drill Progression

Add a third opponent and play 5v3. One player at a time must remain in the restricted zone marked out in the middle of the field. All three players can be out of the zone when trying to score a goal (Fig. 5.13).

Fig. 5.13

Drill Variation

- Defenders score by passing the ball from the halfway line through one of three sets of small goals placed 15 yards inside the opponents' half.

Coaching Interventions

Problem

The team does not advance the ball upfield.

Possible Cause: The players are too risky or too safe passing the ball.

Practice Intervention: *Freeze—Stop the drill and explain to supportive players when to drop back and when to step forward ahead of the ball to receive a pass. Players should dribble forward until they are under pressure by the opponents. *Direct—As the ball approaches the player, the coach can direct the player to "look for passes forward." The coach should remind players not to use square passes.

Other Exercise

Light Pressure, End Zone-Possession Game: 4v2—Moderate Difficulty

The four players score by dribbling into the end zone past the two opponents or by completing ten passes. The two opponents score by making three consecutive passes (Fig. 5.14).

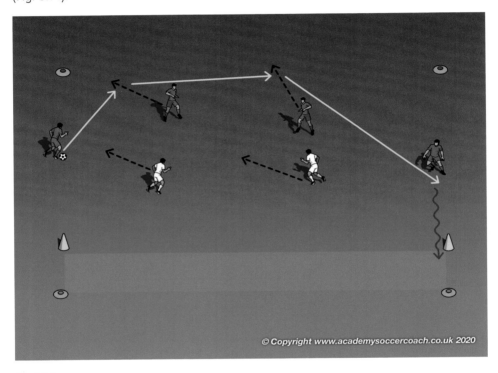

© Copyright www.academysoccercoach.co.uk 2020

Fig. 5.14

Drill Variation

- Only allow one opponent at a time to leave a restricted zone marked out in the center of the field to make it easier to keep possession.

Phase of Play	Build-Up
Coaching Element	#1 Passing Around Light Pressure
Development Stage	IV Standard Game
Drill	"11v11"

Learning Objective

The teams learn how to build up from the back against light pressure in a standard game environment.

Drill Description

4-3-3 v 4-3-3

When a team builds out of the back, the defending team can only pressure with two players and must keep the remaining players near the halfway line. Whenever the ball goes out of play, restart the ball with a goalkeeper so teams have more opportunities to build out of the back under light pressure. Play half of the game with these modified rules before letting the teams play without any modifications for the remainder of the practice.

Player Principles

1.9 Once the goalkeeper collects the ball, the defenders should quickly "spread out wide and deep"—to receive a pass from the goalkeeper.

Defenders should quickly drop into a supportive position in order to create the space to receive a pass from the goalkeeper while facing up the field.

1.10 The goalkeeper should "play defenders to their front foot" (i.e., second foot) when the defenders have space and are looking up the field.

It can be a common problem for goalkeepers to roll or pass the ball out to a defender who might be in the process of getting into a wide position but is still facing the goalkeeper and positioned too centrally. When defenders receive a pass while facing their goalkeeper, they are in a very vulnerable position for having the ball stolen close to the goal with few covering players in place for support (Fig. 5.15).

Fig. 5.15

Coaching Interventions

Problem

The defenders are under too much pressure when they receive the goalkeeper's pass to play the ball out safely.

Possible Cause: The goalkeeper is distributing the ball too early, when the defenders are under pressure or the defenders are facing the goalkeeper and not opened up to the field.

Practice Intervention: *Freeze—Stop the game and explain to the goalkeepers why they need to be patient and wait for defenders to get wide before distributing the ball to them. Goalkeepers have six seconds to distribute the ball once they have control of it in their hands. The coach should count the six seconds out loud so the goalkeeper gets a sense of how long to hold the ball. The goalkeeper should also be told to communicate to the defenders who are slow to transition that they should get wide in supportive positions. *Direct—As the ball is coming under the control of the goalkeeper, remind the goalkeeper to hold the ball and wait for the defenders to get into wide and open positions.

Alternate Formations

9v9 Formation
(4-1-3) v (4-1-3)

In a 9v9 game, teams play with four defenders in the back to encourage building out of the back. When the goalkeeper has the ball, the opposing team should commit two players to win the ball against the team building up from the back.

7v7 Formation
(3-2-1) v (3-2-1)

The teams use three defenders to bring the ball up the field against one opponent allowed to pressure the ball.

5v5 Formation
(2-1-1) v (2-1-1)

The teams build up out of the back with two defenders and the goalkeeper against one pressuring forward.

Skills for Passing Around Pressure

Push Pass

The push pass is the primary way soccer players pass the ball to each other. This skill is difficult to learn correctly because the passing leg and foot are put in an awkward position to make the pass.

1 Soccer Position

"Stand with your feet facing forward, knees softly bent, feet just wider than shoulder width, engaged at the core" (Fig. 3.1, *a* and *b*).

2 Grounded Skill Position

"Turn your passing foot perpendicular to the planted foot with your passing foot still on the ground. The heel of the passing foot is about the width of a closed fist away from the inside of the planting foot. Knees are bent and the toe of the planted leg should point straight at the target" (Fig. 5.16*a*).

3 Open Skill Position

a) "Lift your passing foot in the air a couple of inches in the same position as it was on the ground. Ensure the planting knee stays bent as you lift up the passing foot" (Fig. 5.16*b*).

Fig. 5.16a

Fig. 5.16b

b) "Swing the passing foot up and back straight in front of you and not at an angle. The passing foot should move about two inches above the ground. The passing movement should be smooth. Keep the planting knee bent" (Fig. 5.16c).

Fig. 5.16c

Troubleshooting

The passing foot is too high off the ground when swinging up and back.

"Crunch at your core to lower your center of gravity and bend the planting leg."

The foot does not swing straight up and back, but at an angle.

"Make sure the toe of the planting foot is pointed straight ahead and your planting leg is bent."

c) "Jog three or four steps in place before planting and performing the correct motion of the push pass. Practice the swing of the push pass with both feet."

d) "Jog around the field and perform the motion of the push pass before jogging to a new spot to do another push pass."

The body is out of alignment when making the push pass.

"Make sure you stop your body completely before doing the push pass."

4 Skill

"Pass a ball back and forth with your partner. Use two touches, one to trap and one to pass."

Troubleshooting

The ball is not trapped properly to make a pass with the second touch.

"Trap the ball with the same part of the foot that you use to pass the ball, giving a little when the ball strikes the inside of the foot. The ankle of the trapping foot should remain firm when the foot meets the ball slightly in front of you. The ball should stop in front of you so you can more quickly pass the ball without needing to take another touch on the ball."

Roll Back

The roll back is one of the first dribble moves soccer players should learn. While players naturally want to force the ball forward, the roll back gives players the ability to easily and quickly turn away from pressure, which helps them break the instinct to always play directly toward goal.

1 Soccer Position

"Stand with your feet facing forward, knees softly bent, feet just wider than shoulder width, engaged at the core" (Fig. 3.1, *a* and *b*).

2 Open Skill Position

a) "Place the front part of the sole of your foot on the ball. Press firmly down on the ball and roll it back and forth a few inches to get a feel for it" (Fig. 5.17).

Fig. 5.17

3 Skill

a) "Roll the ball with the sole of your foot directly behind you, turning with the ball so you face the opposite direction. Do not stop the ball as it rolls behind you—let it roll" (Fig. 5.18).

b) "Dribble around the area and perform a roll back."

c) "Perform the roll back and accelerate in the new direction."

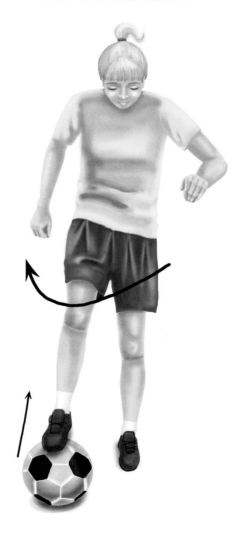

Fig. 5.18

Troubleshooting

Players stop the ball before it has rolled completely behind them.

While the player is performing the turn, tell the player to "let the ball roll" right after the player performs the roll back. Allowing the ball to roll all the way behind them will allow players to more quickly turn around and face the other direction.

Squib Pass

The squib pass is an advanced way to pass the ball accurately on the ground over a longer distance than can be done with a push pass. The pass is completed with the player's foot at a right angle to the ball. This kicking angle allows for more power as the leg can swing more freely.

1 Soccer Position

"Stand with your feet facing forward, knees softly bent, feet just wider than shoulder width, engaged at the core" (Fig. 3.1, *a* and *b*).

2 Grounded Skill Position

"Reach your passing leg out to the side and place your toe on the ground with the knee angled inward. Imagine your foot wrapping around the ball" (Fig. 5.19*a*).

Fig. 5.19a

3 Open Skill Position

"Lift your passing foot with the full instep behind the ball, so the heel stays above the ball" (Fig. 5.19*b*).

Fig. 5.19b

4 Skill

a) "Take a few steps toward a stationary ball and pass it to your partner. The ball should skim along the ground."

b) "Perform the squib pass with the ball moving."

Troubleshooting

The ball goes too high in the air and does not skim along the ground.

"Get your heel higher, so more of your foot is above the ball."

COACHING ELEMENT #2 PASSING THROUGH MODERATE PRESSURE

Paul Pogba of France turns upfield under pressure.

Phase of Play	Build-Up
Coaching Element	#2 Passing Through Moderate Pressure
Development Stage	I Skills and Tactics
Drill	"Triangle Passing"

Learning Objective

Players will improve checking toward the ball and trapping with a half-turn across the body.

Drill Description

Three players pass around a triangle. When they check to the ball, players communicate they are open for a pass. The receiving player uses the foot farthest from the player who will receive the next pass to trap the ball across the body. The third player should move away from the cone to open up space. Players do not follow their passes (Fig. 5.20).

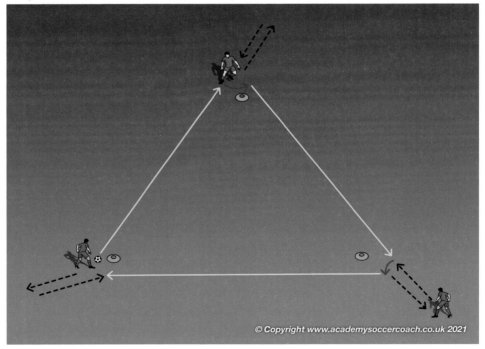

Fig. 5.20

Player Principles
2.1 Players need to "make space."

Players move away from the cone to create space to check into before receiving a pass. Players should keep their "heads on a swivel" when not in possession of the ball, in order to monitor the movements and passing of the other players and to know when to check back to the ball.

2.2 Players need to "create surprise" when they check to the ball.

The timing of checking to the ball is essential when the receiver is tightly marked by an opponent. In a game, if the player checks to the ball too early and has to wait for the pass, the opponent will have time to recover and defend against the pass. If the player checks too late, there will not be enough space to trap the pass. When the player checks at the right time, the defender will not be able to maintain close contact and the receiver will have time and space to trap the ball across the body and look up the field.

2.3 Players need to "protect the ball" when they make the trap.

When the pass is played to the receiver's right foot, then the inside of the right foot is used to trap the ball across the left planting foot. With the trap, the inside of the right foot slightly curls the ball around the left planting foot. A full turn is not completed with the first touch to ensure the ball is kept protected. In a game, a second touch will be needed to turn all the way around. As players receive the ball, they can fake that they are going to turn directly upfield by pivoting in that direction, before trapping the ball across the body in the opposite direction. When building up from the back through the midfield, players want to keep the ball protected because an easy giveaway could lead to a quick counterattack for the opponents.

2.4 Players need to "look up" after they trap the ball in order to find the next pass.

After the player traps the ball with the protected half-turn, then the player needs to look up to cue the next player to check to the pass. The receiver should not check to the ball until eye contact has been made with the passer.

Skills Introduced

Trapping

- Half-turn (protective) across the body

Passing

- Timed passes to the protective foot, away from defensive pressure
- One-touch passing across the body

Tactics

- Checking away from and to the ball

Drill Progression

1. Receive with the inside of the right foot while passing clockwise.
2. Pass counterclockwise and receive with the inside of the left foot.
3. Passing counterclockwise, trap with the outside of the right foot, which crosses the body in front of the left foot.
4. Passing clockwise, trap with the outside of the left foot, which crosses the body in front of the right foot.
5. Check to the ball as if trapping with the protected right foot, but instead make a one-touch pass to the next player with the inside of the right foot across the body.

Drill Variations

- Make the triangle larger.
- Add a second player to each cone, so the checking player has someone to push against when making space. (Players switch roles after every pass or every few minutes so both players have a chance to practice trapping.) The checking player needs to be shown how to push away a defender with the arm close to the body. The arm closest to the defender acts like a "feeler"—letting the attacking player know the whereabouts of the defender.

Note: Do not have players change positions around the triangle after each pass, since you want them to get used to having a certain position on the field where they "create and use space." There is less interchange of positions with build-up. Rather, players occupy certain areas of the field that they attempt to exploit.

Coaching Interventions

Problem

The players control the ball at an angle that does not allow them to pass directly to the next person without passing through the triangle.

Possible Cause #1 The receiving player checks too early and ends up too close to the passer.

Practice Intervention: *Freeze—Make sure the receiver of the pass knows to make eye contact with the passer before checking toward the ball. Moving toward the ball before the passer looks up often results in the receiver getting too close to the passer. Players should rehearse the correct movement.

Possible Cause #2: The receiving player did not create enough space to check to the ball.

Practice Intervention: *Freeze—Explain to the player the importance of "making space to use space" in a game. Show the players how far from the cone they must go to create enough space to check into and have players rehearse the correct run. *Drill Change— Place a poly spot marker that the players have to check back to in between passes. *Direct—After the player passes the ball, remind the player to make space by checking away from the cone, especially when the player tends to drift toward the passer.

Possible Cause #3: The passer looked up and made eye contact with the receiver but did not pass immediately, and instead took another touch on the ball.

Practice Intervention: *Direct—Tell the players while the ball is traveling to them that they should play quickly after they trap the ball and not take extra touches.

Possible Cause #4: The receiving player did not use the right technique to trap the ball all the way across the body.

Practice Intervention: *Freeze—Show the proper technique for trapping the ball by using a firm ankle with a slight snap so the ball is brought across the body away from the passer. The snapping movement is done quickly and at the last moment for an element of surprise. There should be a slight side spin on the ball to help it stay close to the receiving player as it curls across the body. Players should practice the proper technique prior to restarting the drill.

Competitive Game

Triangle Passing Competition—Easy Drill
Every group does the triangle passing Drill and the coach judges which group does it the best.

Other Exercises

Half-Turn Passing Pattern—Moderate Difficulty
Player 1 and player A start passing in opposite directions. When the player on the ball traps the ball across the body and looks up, then the next player on the opposite side checks to the ball and calls for a pass. Player 1 passes to player 2, player 2 to 3, 3 to 4 and then straight across to player 5 who passes back in the opposite direction to player 6, etc. Players can follow their passes to the next cone, or they can check back and forth from the same cone (Fig. 5.21).

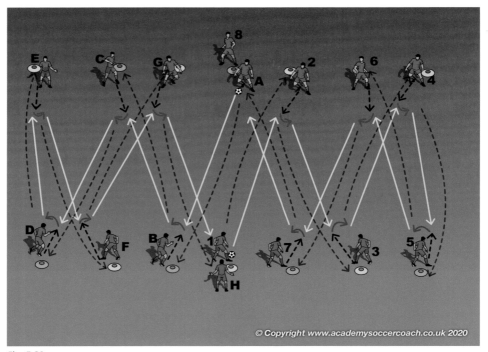

Fig. 5.21

Half-Turn Passing Back to Partner—Easy Drill

Player 1 looks up with the ball, which is the cue for player 2 to check to the centerline to receive the ball across the body, turn and pass to player 3. If the pass is played to the left side of player 2, the player turns with the inside of the left foot across the body to the player's right side. If it is played to the right side of player 2, the receiver uses the inside of the right foot to turn the ball across the body to the left side. When player 3 receives the ball and looks up, player 1 is cued to check to the ball and do a half-turn and pass back to player 4 (Fig. 5.22).

Fig. 5.22

Half-Turns in Open Space—Easy Drill

Half the players are inside and half the players are outside the rectangular playing area. Half of the outside players have a ball. The players inside the rectangle are in pairs. One player checks to someone on the outside for a pass, completes a half-turn and passes to another player on the outside of the area who does not have a ball. The partner of the player turning with the ball defends with moderate pressure. Both players return to the center between passes. Switch player roles every few minutes (Fig. 5.23).

Fig. 5.23

Competitive Transition Half-Turn Game in Open Space—Moderate Difficulty

The players are in the same configuration as in the previous drill ("Half-Turns in Open Space"). In this competitive game, one player from each pair attempts to make as many half-turns and passes to open players on the outside as possible in one minute, always returning to the center before checking to another player on the outside with a ball. The player's partner attempts to stop the turn and pass from happening. Players get one point for every half-turn and completed pass. Play each round for one minute.

Directional Half-Turn Passing Pattern—Advanced Drill

Player 1 (representing the left center back) passes to player 2's (representing the left fullback) right foot. Player 2 checks to the ball and does a half-turn toward the inside of the field. Player 2 passes to the left foot of player 3 (representing the center defensive midfielder), who does a half-turn and passes to player 4 (representing the left wing forward). Player 4 checks to the ball and traps with the right foot toward the center of the field and passes to player 5 (representing a center forward/attacking mid). The passing pattern continues down the other side of the field. Player 5 then plays to player 6, who has checked to the ball to do a half-turn with the right foot toward the center of the field. After passing the ball, the players drop back into their original starting positions to create space to check into for the next pass. There is no interchanging of positions (Fig. 5.24).

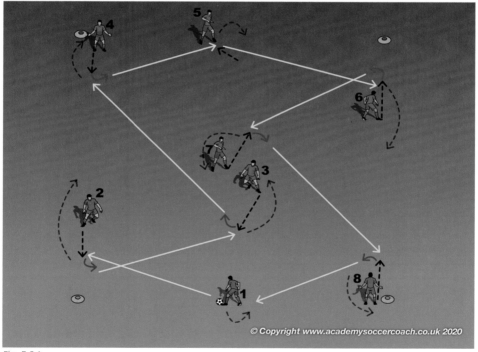

Fig. 5.24

Drill Progression

1. Add a second ball once the players understand the pattern, with player 1 and player 5 starting the passing pattern at the same time.

2. Instead of trapping the ball, players make a one-touch pass across their bodies.

Drill Variation

- Add one more player to players 2, 6, 4, 8, 7, and 3, who apply moderate pressure without trying to get the ball. For example, player 2 would push away the defensive player before checking to the ball in the space created. After each pass (or after one to two minutes) the partners switch roles.

Positional Half-Turn Passing Pattern—Advanced Drill

The goalkeeper starts the drill and plays to player 1, who is in an open position and receives with the second foot. Player 1 passes to player 2 checking to the ball, player 2 does a half-turn and passes to player 3 checking to the ball. Player 3 does a half-turn and passes to player 4 checking to the ball, player 4 does a half-turn and passes to player 5 who has opened up in a supportive position. Player 5 passes to player 6 who is checking to the ball. Player 6 does a half-turn and plays a lofted ball back to the goalkeeper, who begins the drill again with a pass to player 1. The same passing pattern is performed on the other side of the field with the goalkeeper passing to player A (Fig. 5.25).

Fig. 5.25

Drill Variations

- Add defensive players who offer passive resistance to the passers. The player passing would push the defensive player away before checking to the ball. After each round, the partners would switch. It is best if defensive players partner with players 2/B, 3/C, 4/D, and 6/F. In this drill, players 1/A and 5/E drop behind the ball and trap with the second foot, rather than trapping in a protective way across the body.
- Add a third or fourth ball to speed up play.
- Add a second goalkeeper.

Two-Player Half-Turn Drill—Easy Drill

Each player stands behind a line marked out by cones. Player 1 checks past the line toward player 2, who passes the ball to the right foot of player 1. Player 1 does a half-turn and dribbles a couple of yards before turning back and returning to the spot where the trap was made. Meanwhile, player 2 has moved away as player 1 was dribbling. Once player 1 returns to the original spot with the ball, player 2 checks towards the passer and receives a pass from player 1 on the left foot. Player 2 performs a half-turn to the right side and repeats the drill. Players alternate trapping in each direction (Fig. 5.26).

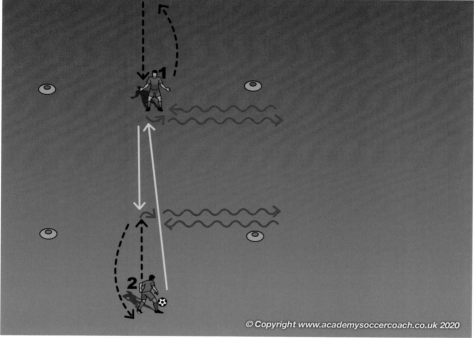

© Copyright www.academysoccercoach.co.uk 2020

Fig. 5.26

One-Player Half-Turn Drill—Easy Drill

The player passes the ball against a wall, checks to the ball, and uses a half-turn to take the ball to one side or the other. After the turn, the player dribbles a short distance before turning and dribbling back to perform another pass against the wall and a half-turn in the opposite direction (Fig. 5.27).

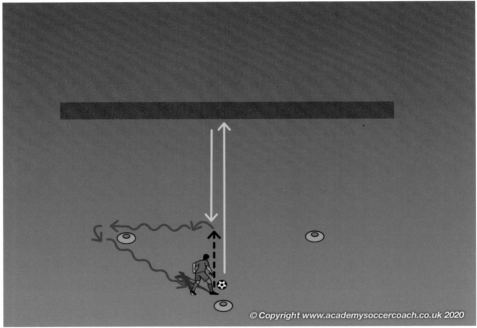

Fig. 5.27

Phase of Play	Build-Up
Coaching Element	#2 Passing Through Moderate Pressure
Development Stage	II Competitive Game
Drill	"3v3 + 4 Half-Turn Possession Game"

Learning Objective

Players will learn how to utilize half-turns across the body to protect the ball from pressure and find open teammates.

Drill Description

3v3+4

A team of three players competes against another team of three players in a square area with four bumpers who play with the team in possession. The goal is to make five consecutive passes, or to switch the field directly from one side to the opposite side—in any direction. The five passes include passes to and from the bumpers. In order to force half-turns, players are not allowed to pass back to the bumpers who pass to them. When the defending team wins the ball, they become attackers and attempt to make five passes or to switch the field. The two teams man-mark each other. Rotate the bumper players into the center after three to four minutes (Fig. 5.28).

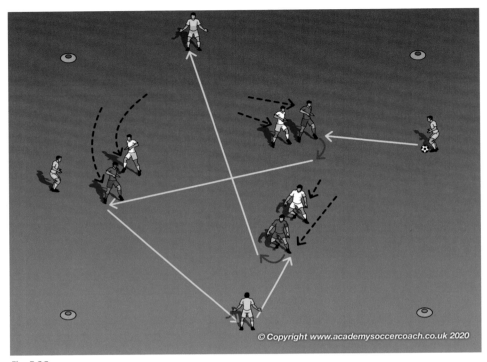

Fig. 5.28

Player Principles

2.5 The player receiving the pass should "trap the ball away from pressure."

When receiving the ball, the receiving player needs to be aware of the defender's position to know which way to turn.

2.6 Supporting players tell the receiver of the pass, "Man on" or "Turn."

As the pass is traveling toward a receiver, supporting players should communicate whether there is space to turn.

2.7 The players checking to the ball should "communicate with the passer" to indicate that they want the ball passed to them at that moment.

The timing of the checking needs to be in sync with the passing. The player who is open to receiving a pass can indicate being open in several ways:

- Calling out "Here."
- Saying the name of the passer.
- Use of arm signals that can also indicate where the ball should be passed.
- Showing facial expressions, like making one's eyes bigger to indicate readiness to receive a pass.

Drill Variations

- Play 4v4+4.
- Enlarge or shrink the playing space.
- Make the playing field a rectangle with points only given for switching play lengthwise.
- Restrict the bumpers to one or two touches/seconds with the ball.
- Encourage turning and switching the field by adding extra points when these are completed.

Coaching Interventions

Problem

Teams are not able to keep possession or switch sides.

Possible Cause #1: Passes are made too early or too late, evident by the defender winning the ball from the receiver when the pass is made.

Practice Intervention: *Explain—Between games, discuss how the passer should wait for eye contact with the receiver before making the pass. The receiving player needs to check quickly after the player on the ball looks up. A player standing open but looking away is not open, and a pass should not be made to that player until there is eye contact. *Direct—Coach the player within the game to pass the ball at the right time when the receiver is checking to the ball.

Possible Cause #2: Passes are made to the wrong foot of the receiver.

Practice Intervention: *Demonstrate—Between games, show the reason for passing the ball to the foot of the receiver farthest away from pressure. Coach the receiver to communicate where the ball should be played—for example, by pointing to the foot where the pass should be made while checking to the ball.

Possible Cause #3: Players do not communicate.

Practice Intervention: *Direct—Tell players within the game that they need to talk to one another. An open player needs to communicate being open, and the player making the pass and other teammates need to tell the receiving player "Turn" or "Man on," so the receiving player knows what to do when trapping the ball.

Possible Cause #4: Players off the ball are too close or too far away from the passer.

Practice Intervention: *Demonstrate—Between games, put players in different places on the field to show what is too far or too close to the ball. *Direct—At key moments, coach players to be more aware of their positioning in relationship to the ball.

Other Exercises

3v3+4 Positional Half-Turn Possession Game—Moderate Difficulty

This drill should be performed between the penalty box and the halfway line, where the three midfielders mostly play when building up in a 4-3-3 formation. One rule change is that a team can get a point with seven passes or turning and passing to the player acting as the center forward (CF), giving the drill direction (Fig. 5.29).

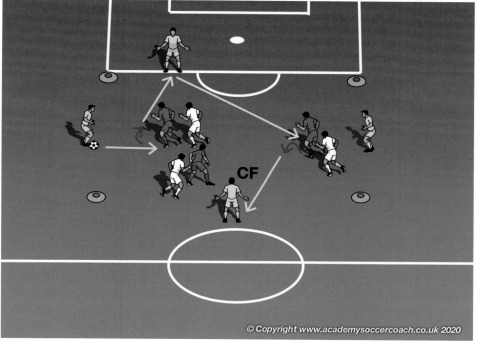

Fig. 5.29

8v4 Half-Turn Possession Game with Goals—Moderate Difficulty

Eight players keep possession from the four defenders. The eight players score by completing ten passes consecutively or when one of the central players can turn and pass the ball between two defenders, i.e., "splitting the defense." The four defenders score by winning the ball and scoring in either goal (Fig. 5.30).

Note: Adding the goals creates transitional moments when attackers have to adjust from an expanded position to a compact position to defend the goals and win the ball back.

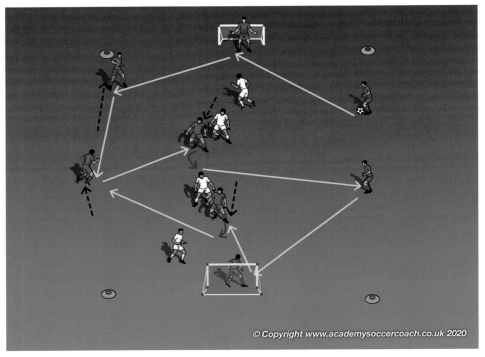

Fig. 5.30

Drill Variations

- The defending team can also score by making three consecutive passes.
- The defending team can only send three players at a time into one half of the field, in order to make it easier for the attackers to link passes.

11v6 Positional Half-Turn Possession Game—Advanced Drill

Play in one half of the field. The team of 11 makes 8 to 12 passes for a point or completes a half-turn under pressure and plays the ball upfield to a teammate. The defending team of six scores on the goal or makes four passes for a point (Fig. 5.31).

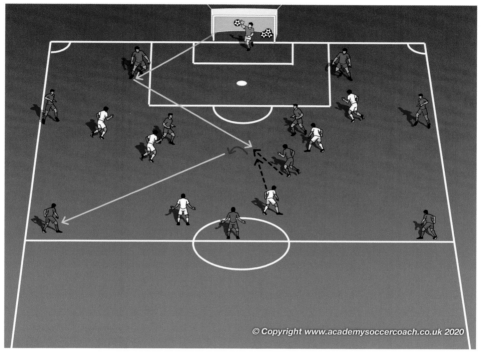

Fig. 5.31

Phase of Play	Build-Up
Coaching Element	#2 Passing Through Moderate Pressure
Development Stage	III Positional Game
Drill	"11v8 Build-Up Under Moderate Pressure With Transition to Attack"

Learning Objective

Players will learn how to build up out of their defensive half under moderate pressure.

Drill Description

11v8

The attacking team plays out from the goalkeeper and scores by passing the ball through the midfield until the team can pass to a forward moving into the end zone. The attacking team can also score by making 10 consecutive passes. The defending team of 8 scores on the goal (Fig. 5.32).

Fig. 5.32

Player Principles

2.8 Players "communicate with the pass."

The weight and direction of a pass to a receiver are dictated by the positioning of the receiver and the opponent guarding the receiver. The pass can be heavy, firm, or soft and directed to the receiver's left or right side. The way the passer passes the ball to the receiver can communicate to the receiver what type of trap to use.

For example, when a receiver is checking back to the ball from an advanced position, then a firm pass to the foot closest to the sideline can communicate that the player is under pressure and needs to protect the ball (see Figs. 5.33, *a* and *b*).

Fig. 5.33a

Fig. 5.33b

When players are in a supportive position, then a firm pass to the foot closest to the sideline can also indicate that the player should protect the ball by staying wide (Fig. 5.33c).

Fig. 5.33c

On the other hand, passing to the receiver's foot closest to the center of the field will allow both the supportive player and the player checking back to the ball the opportunity to more easily go forward with the ball toward the opposing team's goal (Figs. 5.33, *d* and *e*). This is possible when the receiver is under light or no pressure.

Fig. 5.33, d and e

2.9 "Make the field as large as possible."

When bringing the ball forward out of their half, players should make the field as big as possible by occupying the edges in order to create room and space to check to the ball and make half-turns upfield.

Coaching Interventions

Problem

The attacking team is unable to find forward passes to advance the ball up the field.

Possible Cause: The players are clumping.

Practice Intervention: *Freezing—Stop the game and show that checking too early or drifting absentmindedly toward the ball will crowd vital spaces required for checking. Players need to be patient in their positions, and only check to the ball when the passer looks up to make a pass. Reinforce these points at restarts. *Direct—Within the run of play, remind players to hold their positions and wait for the right moment to check to the ball. *Drill Change—Adjust the practice parameters to support player learning—remove or add defensive players, change player matchups, and change the scoring system.

Phase of Play	Build-Up
Coaching Element	#2 Passing Through Moderate Pressure
Development Stage	IV Standard Game
Drill	"11v11"

Learning Objective

The attacking team will learn to build up from the back under moderate pressure in a standard game environment.

Drill Description
4-3-3 v 4-3-3

In build-up, the fullbacks and center midfielders are under moderate pressure. The ball restarts with the goalkeeper after the ball goes out of bounds for the first half. In the second half, there are no special rules.

Player Principle

2.10 Players need to take initiative and check to the ball and do half-turns under moderate pressure.

Coaching Interventions

Problem

The team does not try to advance the ball upfield while passing on the ground.

Possible Cause: Players are afraid to turn under moderate pressure, and continue to pass back until a player has to kick the ball directly upfield.

Practice Intervention: *Direct—Players need encouragement to receive the ball with a half-turn. Players should be praised for trying to do half-turns, even if they lose the ball, since this is a difficult skill to perfect. *Freeze—Stop the game to show when players should pass through the midfield in build-up and when they should play safer and try to work the ball around pressure.

Alternate Formations

9v9 Formation
(4-3-1) v (4-3-1)

Each team has four fullbacks and three midfielders to work on building out of the back under moderate pressure.

7v7 Formation
(2-3-1) v (2-3-1)

The two fullbacks split wide and pass forward through the three midfielders.

5v5 Formation
(2-1-1) v (2-1-1)

The two fullbacks split wide and look to pass to the center midfielder or forward, who are checking to the ball.

COACHING ELEMENT #3 PASSING OVER HEAVY PRESSURE

The French national team player Olivier Giroud traps a long pass under pressure.

Phase of Play	Build-Up
Coaching Element	#3 Passing Over Heavy Pressure
Development Stage	I Skills and Tactics
Drill	"Long Passing Pattern"

Learning Objective

Players will improve their ability to make long passes on the ground and in the air. Players will also learn how to trap longer passes in a variety of ways.

Drill Description

Players pass to the receiving player and follow their passes. The initial passes are on the ground. As players warm up, the passes are made in the air. Move the cones back to make the passes longer. As the passes get longer, players don't follow their passes (Fig. 5.34).

Fig. 5.34

Player Principles

3.1 The longer, lofted pass should have a "gentle backspin on the ball."

Players should strike the ball so that the ball has a slight backspin to ensure the pass is stable, does not knuckle, and is easier to control. A spin to the side will curve the ball away from the receiver and make trapping the ball harder since the pass will be more difficult to judge.

3.2 A squib pass should "skim the surface of the ground" so the ball can travel faster over a longer distance.

Players passing the ball long on the ground should aim for the ball to skip along the surface so that it is almost rolling when it reaches its target.

3.3 The receiver of a long, lofted pass needs to: "first, assess the flight of the ball; second, make a decision how to receive it; and third, move into a position to trap the ball."

Players who receive a long pass often make the mistake of running toward the ball before they have had a chance to assess where the ball will land. This premature reaction can result in the ball going over the player's head or arriving at an awkward angle.

3.4 The receiver should "settle the ball to the ground" as quickly as possible after receiving the pass in the air.

Players must bring the ball down onto the field as quickly as possible with the inside, outside, sole, or top of the foot so they can quickly make the next pass.

Skills Introduced

Trapping

- Inside-of-the-foot trap
- Outside-of-the-foot trap
- Head
- Thigh
- Chest

- Sole-of-the-foot roof trap
- Inside-of-the-foot roof trap
- Outside-of-the-foot roof trap
- Top-of-the-foot roof trap

Passing

- Clipping/driving in the air
- Inside-of-the-foot volley pass
- Outside-of-the-foot volley pass
- Chest pass
- Head pass

Drill Progression

1. Players begin with a long push pass.
2. Pass with a squib passing technique, keeping the ball skipping along the ground to the receiver. The receiver will typically control a squib pass with the inside of the foot.
3. Clip or drive the ball to the receiver from a longer distance. A clipped or driven pass is a long, lofted pass with medium backspin. At first, the ball should be stationary when clipping it, and then it should be moving once the technique has improved.
4. Instead of trapping the ball, the receiver practices "knocking the ball down" to a teammate with one touch, using the inside or outside of the foot, chest or head. The two players alternate roles.

Drill Variations

- Players pass with their non-dominant foot.
- Players aim for the receiver's head, chest, thigh or foot when driving the ball, to work on accuracy.
- Players are encouraged to control the ball and pass more quickly.
- A passive defender can be put behind the receiver, so the receiver has to trap or one-touch pass the ball with moderate pressure.

Trapping Drills

In these drills, practice the following trapping and passing skills: inside-of-the-foot, top-of-the-foot, outside-of-the-foot, thigh, chest, head, and the roof trap, which can be done with the sole, inside and outside of the foot.

Checking and Trapping—Moderate Difficulty

a) Players check to their partners and perform a skill (trapping, volleying) and then check away after passing back to their partners (Fig. 5.35a).

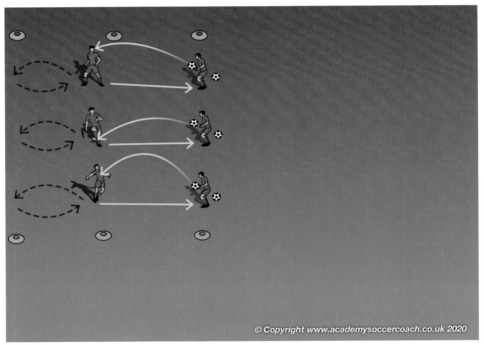

Fig. 5.35a

b) A variation of this drill is for the thrower to backpedal and toss the ball to the player performing the skill, who moves forward. Partners work across the field and switch tossing the ball when they return. It is important in both drills that the trapper comes to a full stop to do the skill before moving forward again. Moving while trying to trap or volley the ball will lead to poor skill development (Fig. 5.35*b*).

Fig. 5.35b

Short-Short-Long Trapping and Volleying—Advanced Drill

Groups of three players volley the ball in a short-short-long sequence to one another, with or without interchanging positions. Players can be told to use only one, two, or more than three touches at a time (Fig. 5.36).

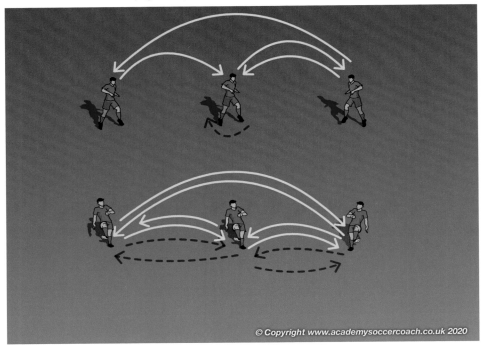

Fig. 5.36

Sequential Trapping—Moderate

Players throw or kick the ball straight up into the air, then perform a series of traps:

1. Kick, catch (practice proper instep kicking technique)
2. 1x thigh catch (drop the ball on the flat thigh and catch it as it comes back up)
3. Thigh juggling (as many as possible)
4. Kick/throw, thigh, catch
5. Kick/throw, sole-of-the-foot roof trap
6. Kick/throw, inside-of-the-foot roof trap
7. Kick/throw, outside-of-the-foot roof trap
8. Kick/throw, alternate roof traps

9. Kick/throw, thigh, any roof trap
10. Kick/throw, head, any roof trap
11. Kick/throw, chest, any roof trap
12. Kick/throw, head, thigh, any roof trap
13. Kick/throw, head, chest, thigh, any roof trap

Note: Advanced players can kick the ball with their instep so that the ball has no spin and goes straight up into the air. Kicking in this way deserves its own instruction and practicing.

Coaching Interventions

Problem #1

The passer is not getting loft on the ball.

Possible Cause #1: The player has poor long-passing skills.

Practice Intervention: *Neuromuscular training—Players should practice the right body positions for this technique. If the foot is not angled enough, the player will be striking the ball with too much of the inside of the foot—like in a push pass. Show the player how to "make a wedge" with the foot. The passer might also be striking the ball too high up the instep, where it is the thickest, and so is unable to get under the ball. Tell the passer to "strike the ball lower on the foot—toward the big toe knuckle." It is common for players to want to strike every ball with the top, thicker part of their instep.

Possible Cause #2: The ball used in the drill is too hard or too heavy.

Practice Intervention: *Drill Change—Take some air out of the soccer balls or use lighter balls. If balls are water-logged, wait for them to dry before practicing this technique.

Possible Cause #3: The player is too small or weak to kick the ball with any power.

Practice Intervention: *Drill Change—Make the space smaller between players. Reduce the expectation that players kick the ball very high or far in the air. Focus on the small gains made.

Problem #2

The receiver is not able to bring the ball down to the ground.

Possible Cause #1: The receiver misjudges the pass.

Practice Intervention: *Direct—Tell the player during the drill to follow the sequence "judge, decide, move" when attempting to trap a long pass. Inexperienced players tend to run toward the passer before judging the distance of the pass.

Possible Cause #2: The receiver has poor trapping technique.

Practice Intervention: *Freeze—Show players the correct position of the body at the time of the trap. Remind the players they must use a firm surface that gives a little at the time of impact. The coach can also throw the ball to the receiver a few times to ensure the player has rehearsed the right technique before letting the player receive a longer pass. Show the proper way to settle the ball quickly to the ground with a roof trap or top-of-the-foot trap after the initial trap has been made.

Possible Cause #3: The receiver does not try to settle the ball to the ground.

Practice Intervention: *Direct—Within the drill, remind the receivers, as they receive a long pass, to bring the ball quickly to the ground. (Many players stop the trapping effort once they do the initial trap out of the air, waiting for the ball to stop bouncing before looking to make the next pass.)

Competitive Game

Clipping Game #1—Moderate Difficulty

Two players pass together and compete against the other pairs of players. Each player is in a box made of four cones three steps apart. The players' boxes are about 20 yards from each other to start. The two players work together to complete two good chips and traps in a row, by trapping the ball in the square out of the air. After two consecutive traps in the box, the players can move their boxes farther apart by the width of one box. This is accomplished by moving the front two cones of one box three steps past the back set of cones which now become the front cones. The winning pair will be the ones farthest apart at the end of a certain amount of time, say, 10 minutes (Fig. 5.37).

Fig. 5.37

Other Exercises

Short-Short-Long Passing—Easy Drill

Three players form a group. Player 1 passes short to player 3, who passes back to player 1, who passes a long, lofted ball over player 3 to player 2. Player 1 then switches places with player 3 and receives a short pass from player 2. Player 1 plays the ball one touch back to player 2, who traps the ball and clips the ball over the head of player 1 to player 3 (Fig. 5.38).

Drill Variation: No switching—the central player stays in the middle for a few minutes before switching out.

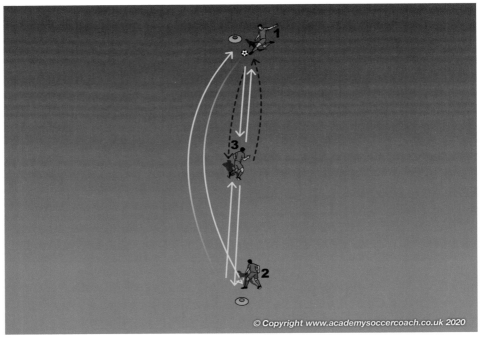

Fig. 5.38

Hourglass—Moderate Difficulty

Six cones are placed in an hourglass shape. Player 1 and player 5 start with the ball. Two players have to be at the cone where the ball is first passed. Players 1 and 5 make a long pass to players 2 and 6, who pass short to players 7 and 3, who pass short to players 8 and 4. All players follow their passes. The hourglass passing pattern allows players to pass at angles that are common in build-up play and provides alternate passing lengths (Fig. 5.39).

Fig. 5.39

Diagonal Redirection—Easy Drill

Players play a lofted ball or a squib pass diagonally and then run to the cone closest to them along the short side of the rectangle, staying out of the center of the field where the passes are made. Players must be alert in order not to hit another person's pass. For increased fitness training, players can switch positions by running (sprinting) along the longer edge (Fig. 5.40).

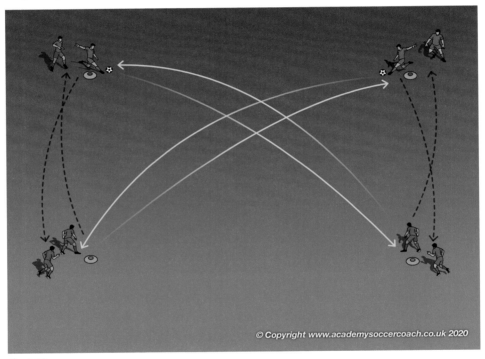

Fig. 5.40

Clipping Game #2—Advanced Drill

Two players compete against each other. Each player makes a 4-yard by 4-yard square from cones about 20 to 30 yards away from each other, depending on the players' ability. One player clips the ball toward the second player in the box, aiming to land the ball in the square. The passer gets a point if the ball lands in the square or the receiving player is unable to trap the ball in the square. If the ball lands outside the square, the receiver gets a point. If the receiver traps the ball in the square, then nobody gets a point. The receiver then clips the ball back.

Phase of Play	Build-Up
Coaching Element	#3 Passing Over Heavy Pressure
Development Stage	II Competitive Game
Drill	"4v2 With a Long Switch"

Learning Objective

Players will learn how to make long passes while under pressure.

Drill Description

Players 1, 2 and 3 keep possession in their half of the field against two opponents with the help of player 4. After five passes, players 1, 2 or 3 can pass to the opposite side to teammates 5 or 6. The possessing team gets one point for making five passes and playing over the halfway line to the two teammates marked by the two defenders. The two marking defenders cannot try to get the ball until the receiving attacker has touched the ball, but they can follow the player if they check to the ball. Once the attacker has attempted to trap the ball, the two defenders attempt to steal the ball from the three attackers plus player 4, who switches sides to offer support. The defenders win the ball and get a point by scoring on goal (Fig. 5.41).

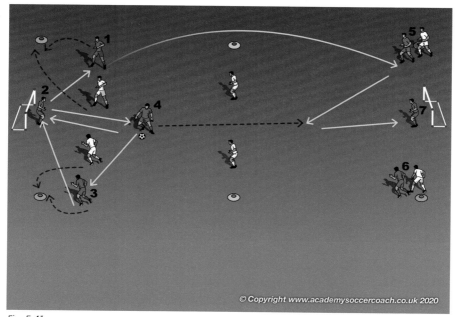

© Copyright www.academysoccercoach.co.uk 2020

Fig. 5.41

Player Principles
3.5 Players "look for seams" to pass and receive the ball.

Under heavy pressure, there is not a lot of space to play safely out of the back, so players must find spaces between the opponents in order to pass the ball upfield.

3.6 Players "choose the right type of pass" over longer distances.

The passer has several options when making a longer pass, such as the clip, squib or push pass. Players need to develop the ability and confidence to choose the correct long-passing approach in any given situation.

Drill Progression
An end zone is added behind each end line. Now the two receivers of the ball can check to the ball or turn and make a run into the end zone to receive a pass if the defender comes too far forward. The end line acts as the offsides line, so the receiving players cannot be in the end zone at the time of the pass. Extra points can be awarded for receiving a pass in the end zone.

Drill Variation
Add two more opponents who stay on the halfway line to make it harder to pass the ball to the players across the field.

Coaching Interventions

Problem
Players are not able to pass the ball across to the other side of the field.

Possible Cause #1: Under the heavy pressure, players are not getting their heads up to look upfield.

Practice Intervention: *Direct—Within the run of play, remind players to look upfield to find passing options, since sometimes players will get too focused on keeping possession.

Possible Cause #2: Players receiving the ball are not finding the seams, checking at the right time, or communicating well enough to the passer that they are free.

Practice Intervention: *Demonstrate—Between games, show the receivers how to get open to receive a pass. The receiving player can check toward or away from the ball to find space, or hold defenders off by leaning toward them at an angle, without moving. *Drill Change—Alter the dimensions of the field or player configurations to make the drill easier.

Phase of Play	Build-Up
Coaching Element #3	Passing Over Heavy Pressure
Development Stage	III Positional Game
Drill	"11v9 Playing Out Under Heavy Pressure"

Learning Objective

Defenders will learn how to build up under heavy pressure by passing directly to the forwards in a game-like environment.

Drill Description

11v9

The team playing out of the defense plays in a 4-3-3 against the opposing team playing in a 3-3-3. All three midfielders and the four defenders can be put under pressure by the opposing team. The defenders will look to pass the ball directly to the forwards over the top or through the opposing team's pressuring players. The forwards can then lay off the ball or trap and turn. The attacking team scores by dribbling over the halfway line, by passing the ball to a teammate who has run into the defending team's half, or by making five consecutive passes. The defending team scores on goal (Fig. 5.42).

Fig. 5.42

Player Principle

3.7 Players need to "anticipate the knockdowns" after long passes to the forwards.

The midfielders need to quickly shift to receive the ball from the forwards when the ball is played directly to the forwards by the defense. When an opponent presses the defenders and the midfielders, then a space generally opens up in front of the forwards where a midfielder could receive a back-pass from a forward.

Drill Variations

- The defending players should mix up how much pressure they put on the full-backs, making the attacking team assess each play to determine the best way to build out of the back.
- The only way to score is to pass the ball to attackers running into the defending team's half—not by dribbling over the halfway line.

Coaching Interventions

Problem

The forwards lose the ball when receiving long passes.

Possible Cause: The forwards do not have any support.

Practice Intervention: *Freeze—Stop the drill and show how midfielders need to anticipate where forwards will need support after a long pass. Midfielders cannot wait for the forwards to trap the pass before moving into a supportive position. Remind players about this important coaching point at restarts. *Direct—Coach midfielders within the game when to provide support to the forwards receiving the ball.

Phase of Play	Build-Up
Coaching Element	#3 Passing Over Heavy Pressure
Development Stage	IV Standard Game
Drill	"11v11"

Learning Objective

The attacking team will practice bringing the ball out of the back under heavy pressure, using long passes directly to the forwards from the defenders.

Drill Description

4-3-3 v 4-3-3

Two teams will play 11v11 on a full field. For the first half of the game, goalkeepers should play the ball out of the back at every restart to increase the number of opportunities to build out of the back. Forwards should be encouraged to press the defenders when the defenders have the ball. In the second half, normal game rules apply.

Player Principle

3.8 Players need to learn how to "read the defense."

The attacking team needs to recognize when to pass directly to the attackers and when to use other build-up approaches.

Coaching Interventions

Problem

The attacking team loses possession advancing the ball out of their half.

Possible Cause: The team in possession chooses the wrong type of build-up strategy—for example, choosing to pass long when they could play through the midfielders to advance the ball.

Practice Intervention: *Freeze—Stop the game to review the three ways to build up from the back: to play around opponents, through opponents, or over opponents, based on the type of pressure put on the ball. *Direct—Within the game let players know what kind of pressure they are experiencing to help them make the right decision.

Alternate Formations

9v9 Formation
3-2-3 v 3-2-3

Teams play with three forwards who can be targets for long passes from the three defenders.

7v7 Formation
3-1-2 v 3-1-2

The two forwards are the targets for the three defenders.

5v5 Formation
2-2 v 2-2

Teams have two players in the back who can pass long to the two forwards.

Skills for Passing Over Heavy Pressure

Sole-of-the-Foot Roof Trap
The sole-of-the-foot roof trap is one of three "roof traps" that players should learn to quickly settle to the ground a ball that would otherwise bounce up into the air without player intervention. These traps are especially useful on harder surfaces such as field turf.

The sole-of-the-foot trap is an ideal trap to settle the ball on the ground when the intention is for the ball to settle directly in front of the player. This trap appears simple, but it can be difficult for players to hold the foot over the ball as it bounces up from the ground at the right height and time. Players should learn how to put the foot into the right position without stamping on the ball. Once mastered, though, players will have an elegant way to settle a ball efficiently on the ground in front of them.

1 Soccer Position

"Stand with your feet facing forward, knees softly bent, feet just wider than shoulder width, engaged at the core" (Figs. 3.1, *a* and *b*).

2 Open Skill Position

a) "With both knees slightly bent, lift the trapping foot so the toe points up at an angle with the heel about six inches off the ground and the foot slightly in front of the body" (Fig. 5.43a).

Fig. 5.43a

b) "Visualize a ball landing at your feet. From the soccer position, drop down and move into the sole-of-the-foot roof trapping position with a small adjustment hop."

c) "From the side, throw the ball directly under the trapping foot so the ball goes up and down against the sole of your foot. The trapping foot acts as a 'roof' and allows the ball to bounce off the ground onto the sole of the foot. Do not smash down on the ball and squeeze the ball against the ground—let the ball meet the foot, not the foot the ball" (Fig. 5.43b).

Fig. 5.43b

3 Skill

a) "Toss the ball into the air and bring your foot straight over the ball with a small hop forward right as the ball comes off the ground so the ball hits the stationary sole of the trapping foot. 'Make a roof—not a trash compactor.' The small hop allows for a last-second adjustment to the position of the ball" (Fig. 5.43c).

Fig. 5.43c

b) "Jog around and toss the ball, or kick the ball, into the air and trap it using the sole-of-the-foot roof trap."

c) "Add a short, quick dribble after trapping the ball."

Troubleshooting

Players have the foot too high over the ball when making the trap.

"Bring the foot straight forward over the ball and not around from the side—this helps keep the foot at the right height."

Players smash down on the ball.

"After a small adjustment hop forward, hold the foot off the ground and wait for the ball to hit your foot."

Inside-of-the-Foot Roof Trap
1 Soccer Position

"Stand with your feet facing forward, knees softly bent, feet just wider than shoulder width, engaged at the core" (Figs. 3.1, *a* and *b*).

2 Open Skill Position

a) "From the soccer position, lift your trapping foot in the air directly to your side by pushing your knee inward—making an angled roof with the inside of your foot about a foot off the ground" (Fig. 5.44a).

Fig. 5.44a

b) "Visualize the ball dropping down in front of you. From the soccer position, drop down into the inside-of-the-foot roof trapping position with a small adjustment hop."

c) "Hold your foot in the trapping position and throw the ball directly under your foot so the ball goes up and down against the inside of the foot. The trapping foot is a 'roof' and allows the ball to bounce off the ground onto the foot. Do not let the trapping foot move toward the bouncing ball, but allow the ball to hit the 'roof,' i.e., the inside of the foot."

3 Skill

a) "Toss the ball into the air and bring your foot over the ball with a small hop right as it comes off the ground, so the ball meets the inside of your trapping foot" (Fig. 5.44b).

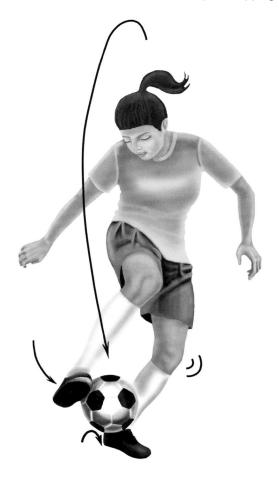

Fig. 5.44b

b) "Jog around and toss or kick your ball into the air and trap the ball using the inside-of-the-foot roof trap, changing directions with the trap."

c) "Add a short, quick dribble after trapping the ball."

Outside-of-the-Foot Roof Trap
1 Soccer Position

"Stand with your feet facing forward, knees softly bent, feet just wider than shoulder width, engaged at the core" (Fig. 3.1, *a* and *b*).

2 Open Skill Position

a) "With your knees deeply bent, bring the trapping foot across in front of your body in order to make a 'roof' with the outside of the foot that is angled and held about 12 inches off the ground. The heel of your trapping foot is almost directly in front of your planting leg" (Fig. 5.45*a*).

Fig. 5.45a

b) "Visualize the ball dropping in front of you. From the soccer position, drop down and move into the outside-of-the-foot trapping position with a small adjustment hop that keeps the trapping foot 12 inches from the ground."

c) "Throw your ball directly under the trapping foot so the ball goes up and down against the outside of the foot. The trapping foot is a 'roof' and allows the ball to bounce off the ground onto the outside of the foot. Do not let the trapping foot move toward the bouncing ball, but allow the ball to hit the roof, i.e., the outside of the foot."

3 Skill

a) "Toss the ball into the air and, with a small adjustment hop, bring your angled foot over the ball right as it comes off the ground, so the ball meets the rigid outside of the trapping foot" (Fig. 5.45b).

Fig. 5.45b

b) "Jog around and toss or kick your ball into the air and trap the ball using the outside-of-the-foot roof trap, changing directions with the trap."

c) "Add a short, quick dribble after trapping the ball."

Top-of-the-Foot Trap
1 Soccer Position

"Stand with your feet facing forward, knees softly bent, feet just wider than shoulder width, engaged at the core" (Fig. 3.1, *a* and *b*).

2 Open Skill Position

a) "Lift your trapping foot a couple of inches off the ground and hold it flat in front of your body so the trapping foot's heel is even with the planting foot's toe" (Fig. 5.46).

Fig. 5.46

b) "Visualize the ball dropping in front of you. From the soccer position, drop down into the top-of-the-foot trapping position with a small adjustment hop."

3 Skill

a) "Throw the ball in the air and let your foot give a bit with a small hop when the ball hits the top of your foot. The ball should come to rest on the ground after a small bounce."

b) "Jog around and toss or kick your ball into the air and trap the ball using the top-of-the-foot roof trap."

c) "Add a short, quick dribble after trapping the ball."

Inside-of-the-Foot Trap
1 Soccer Position

"Stand with your feet facing forward, knees softly bent, feet just wider than shoulder width, engaged at the core" (Fig. 3.1, *a* and *b*).

2 Open Skill Position

a) "Lift your trapping foot in the air and open up your hips so the trapping foot is facing forward with your knee facing away from your body. Your trapping thigh should be parallel to the ground. The inside of the trapping foot is slightly forward and even with the toe of the planting foot, and your trapping foot heel is about 12 inches to the side of the planting leg. The trapping ankle is firm" (Fig. 5.47).

Fig. 5.47

b) "Visualize a long, lofted pass coming toward you. From the soccer position, drop into the inside-of-the-foot trapping position with a small hop. Once the trapping foot is in the air, the foot should give a little, as if receiving the impact of the ball."

3 Skill

a) "One partner throws the ball to the receiver, who traps the ball with the inside of the foot. Your trapping foot should give a little when the ball strikes it, to take energy out of the ball."

b) "The trapper checks to the partner throwing the ball and makes the trap with the inside of the foot."

c) "One partner chips, clips or volleys the ball to the trapper, who receives the pass out of the air with the inside of the foot. After the trap, the receiver chips, clips or volleys the ball back to the partner, who traps the ball the same way."

Passing Variation

- Rather than trapping the ball to the ground, the trapper uses the inside of the foot to volley the ball back to a teammate a few yards away. The same technique is used, but the foot gives less when receiving the ball so the ball is passed back to the teammate.

Outside-of-the-Foot Trap
1 Soccer Position

"Stand with your feet facing forward, knees softly bent, feet just wider than shoulder width, engaged at the core" (Figs. 3.1, *a* and *b*).

2 Open Skill Position

a) "Lift your trapping leg straight up in front of you with a bent knee and turn your trapping foot inward toward the planting leg, so the outside of the foot is facing outward. The trapping foot should be across your body and directly in front of the planting leg. Your ankle should be firm" (Fig. 5.48a).

Fig. 5.48a

b) "Visualize a long, lofted pass is coming toward you. From the soccer position, drop into the outside-of-the-foot trapping position with a small hop. Once the trapping foot is in the right position in the air, the foot should give a little, as if receiving the impact of the pass."

3 Skill

a) "One partner throws the ball to the trapper, who receives the ball out of the air with the outside of the foot" (Fig. 5.48*b*).

Fig. 5.48b

b) "The trapper checks to the ball and makes the trap with the outside of the foot."

c) "One partner chips, clips, or volleys the ball to the trapper, who traps the ball out of the air with the outside of the foot. The receiver then chips, clips, or volleys the ball back to the partner, who traps the ball in the same way."

Passing Variation

- Rather than trapping the ball to the ground, the trapper volleys the ball back to a teammate a few yards away with the outside of the foot. The same technique is used, but the foot gives less when receiving the ball so the ball is passed back to a teammate.

Head Trap

1 Soccer Position

"Stand with your feet facing forward, knees softly bent, feet just wider than shoulder width, engaged at the core" (Figs. 3.1, *a* and *b*).

2 Open Skill Position

a) "Move one leg behind you and one leg forward, so you are in a straddle position with your feet shoulder-width apart and knees bent. Twist the body slightly so one shoulder is more forward while you angle your forehead upward. Keep the chin tucked, mouth closed, and eyes open" (Fig. 5.49*a*).

Fig. 5.49a

b) "Visualize a long, lofted pass is coming toward you. From the soccer position, drop into the head-trapping position with a small adjustment hop."

3 Skill

a) "One partner tosses the ball to the receiver. Perform a small adjustment hop to adjust positioning and bend the knees as the ball strikes the forehead in order to cushion the impact of the ball. Use one of the roof traps or the top-of-the-foot trap to settle the ball to the ground" (Fig. 5.49*b*).

Fig. 5.49b

b) "The trapper checks to the ball and makes the head trap."

c) "One player volleys the ball up into the air to a partner, who traps the ball with the head and settles it with one of the roof traps or the top-of-the-foot trap."

Passing Variation

- Rather than trapping the ball to the feet, the trapper heads the ball back to a teammate a few yards away. The same technique is used, but the head gives less when receiving the ball so the ball is redirected to a teammate.

Chest Trap

1 Soccer Position

"Stand with your feet facing forward, knees softly bent, feet just wider than shoulder width, engaged at the core" (Figs. 3.1, *a* and *b*).

2 Open Skill Position

a) "Place one leg behind you and one leg forward in a straddle position with your feet shoulder-width apart and some give in the knees. Bring the elbows back so the chest is pushed outward and upward. Chin is firmly tucked" (Fig. 5.50*a*).

Fig. 5.50a

b) "Visualize a long, lofted pass coming toward you. From the soccer position, drop into the chest-trapping position with a small adjustment hop."

3 Skill

a) "One partner tosses the ball to the trapper, who performs an adjustment hop and bends the knees as the ball hits the chest right below the chin. The ball should spring up slightly just in front of the chin before dropping to the ground. Use one of the roof traps or the top-of-the-foot trap to settle the ball to the ground" (Fig. 5.50b).

Fig. 5.50b

b) "The trapper checks to the ball and makes the chest trap."

c) "One partner volleys the ball up into the air to the trapper, who traps the ball with the chest and settles it with one of the roof traps or the top-of-the-foot trap."

Passing Variation

- Rather than trapping the ball to the ground, the receiver chests the ball back to a teammate a few yards away. The same technique is used, but the chest moves toward the ball on impact so the ball is redirected to a teammate.

Thigh Trap

1 Soccer Position

"Stand with your feet facing forward, knees softly bent, feet just wider than shoulder width, engaged at the core" (Figs. 3.1, *a* and *b*).

2 Open Skill Position

a) "Lift the trapping thigh so it is flat and parallel with the ground. Bend the supporting knee" (Fig. 5.51*a*).

Fig. 5.51a

b) "Visualize a high ball coming toward you. From the soccer position, drop into a thigh trap position with a slight adjustment hop. Your thigh should give a little as you imagine the ball striking the center of your thigh to reduce the force of the ball."

3 Skill

a) "Practice thigh juggling, hitting the ball in the middle of the thigh."

b) "Toss the ball into the air and give slightly when the ball hits the middle of your thigh. Initially, you should catch the ball in the air with your hands after the ball comes off the thigh. Later, you should use one of the roof traps or the top-of-the-foot trap to settle the ball to the ground" (Fig 5.51b).

Fig. 5.51b

c) "One partner throws the ball to the trapper, who traps the ball with the thigh. Settle the ball to the ground with a roof or top-of-the-foot trap."

d) "Check to the ball and perform the thigh trap."

e) "One partner volleys the ball up in the air to the trapper, who traps the ball with the thigh and settles it with a roof or top-of-the-foot trap."

Long Clipped or Driven Pass

Much practice is required to perfect the clipped or driven pass. The pass should travel with a low arc and a gentle backspin. A ball that knuckles or curves is more difficult to trap. Also, a pass that goes too high in the air will give the opponents time to adjust to the flight of the ball and challenge the receiver. The pass should just be high enough to clear the opponents' heads.

1 Soccer Position

"Stand with your feet facing forward, knees softly bent, feet just wider than shoulder width, engaged at the core" (Figs. 3.1, *a* and *b*).

2 Grounded Skill Position

"Extend the kicking leg out to the side of the body and point the kicking toe outward. Push the kicking foot's knee forward so the instep angles forward, making a wedge with your foot. It should feel awkward and put some strain on the kicking knee. The knees end up being only about 12 inches apart, with the kicking foot's heel about twice that distance away from the heel of the planting foot" (Fig. 5.52, *a* and *b*).

Fig. 5.52, a and b

3 Open Skill Position

"Slightly lift the kicking foot off the ground with the same angle behind the ball" (Fig. 5.52c). Note: In a chip pass, the foot would be as low as possible on the ball.

Fig. 5.52c

4 Skill

a) "Drive the ball back and forth, practicing trapping and settling the ball. The ball should have a slight backspin, allowing the ball to fly straight to your partner. The ball should be stationary when you kick it."

b) "Drive the ball while it is still in motion off the dribble."

Troubleshooting

The ball does not fly straight to the partner.

"Visualize the ball going in a low arc with medium backspin toward your partner."

With continued trouble, the players should practice the grounded and open positions again to remind them of the proper foot positioning and body orientation. Be patient, as this is a difficult skill for players to master.

COACHING ELEMENT #4 PROBING PASSING

picture alliance / dpa | Juan Carlos Cardenas

Real Madrid's Luka Modric looks to create an attack on goal.

Phase of Play	Probing
Coaching Element	#4 Probing Passing
Development Stage	I Skills and Tactics
Drill	"Rondo"

Learning Objective

Players will learn how to keep possession in a tight space using one- and two-touch passing.

Drill Description

5v1

Five players make a tight circle around one defender and, using only one or two touches, keep possession from the defender. The defender switches into the middle after winning the ball or after a certain amount of time. For younger players, the coach can be the defender and apply light pressure (Fig. 5.53).

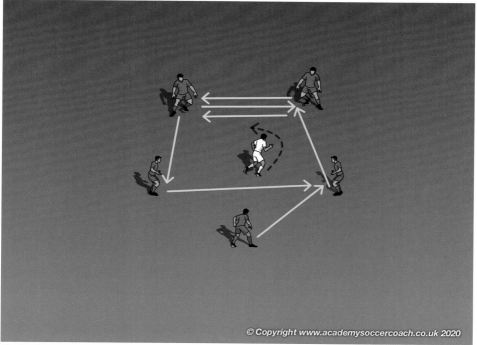

Fig. 5.53

Player Principles

4.1 Passes should be "played to the feet."

In small areas under tight pressure, players need to aim firm passes directly at their teammates' feet, since the receiver will have very little time and space to receive any other type of pass. The weight and accuracy of passes are crucial in these situations.

4.2 Receivers of the pass need to be "on their toes" and ready to make quick passes.

Supporting players need to be ready for unexpected passes, since the ball will move quickly in these passing situations.

Skills Introduced

Passing

- One- and two-touch passing under pressure

Drill Progression

1. Players have two touches to pass the ball.
2. Players play one-touch.
3. A second defender can be added.
4. The playing area can be made smaller.

Coaching Interventions

Problem

The passing is inaccurate.

Possible Cause #1: The receiver is flat-footed.

Practice Intervention: *Direct—During the game, remind players to be "alive and active." Players should never be flat-footed.

Possible Cause #2: The receiver of the pass is not square to the ball.

Practice Intervention: *Freeze—Stop the drill and show how to rotate facing the ball at all times, so the player will not be sideways to the ball and twisted when trying to make a pass.

Possible Cause #3: The passer has poor passing technique.

Practice Intervention: *Neuromuscular training—Players should review the push-passing technique. The pass has to be straight to the feet and have the right weight so the receiver will be able to pass the ball with one touch to the next person. *Direct—During the game, players can be reminded to use the inside of the foot if possible, since it is more accurate than the outside of the foot, which is used sometimes by players who are not square to the pass and are off balance.

Competitive Game

5v1 Rondo Game—Moderate Difficulty

The outside players get a point for seven consecutive passes, while the defender gets a point for stealing the ball and dribbling out of the area. The same rules apply if the game is changed to 5v2.

Other Exercises

10-Pass Challenge—Moderate Difficulty

Two players stand facing each other on a line about 10 yards apart. The goal is for the players to pass one-touch back and forth so the ball is always moving in the direction of the far cones down the line. The challenge is to complete ten passes that move toward the opposite side, i.e., the passes cannot go backward. All ten passes must be completed before reaching the far cones. The distance between passers can be increased or decreased to make the drill easier or harder (Fig. 5.54).

Drill Variation: Once players are able to pass ten times in one direction before reaching the end, the coach can time the players to see how quickly they can complete the ten passes from one side to the other.

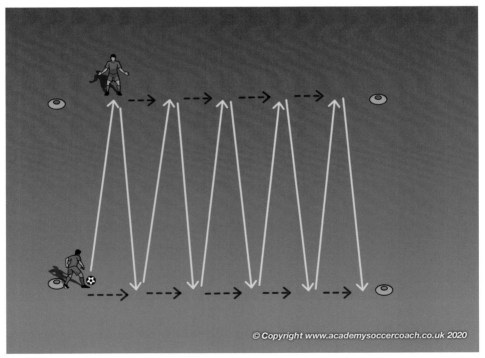

Fig. 5.54

"Cross" Passing Pattern—Easy Drill

Players play one- or two-touch passes and follow their passes in a crossing pattern (Fig. 5.55).

Fig. 5.55

Stationary Passing—Easy Drill

Players stand 5 to 10 yards apart and pass the ball back and forth to each other with one-touch passes. In between passes, players keep light on their toes. As the ball arrives, the passing player must drop down into the passing position with a small adjustment hop, crunch at the core, and firm the ankle. The passer strikes the middle of the ball just in front of the body.

Drill Variation: Players form a circle and pass the ball to each other, one-touch, in random ways. "No-look" or deceptive passing can be added to this drill, where players look one way but pass in another direction.

Circle One-Touch Group Passing—Easy Drill

Half the players are in the larger circle and half the players with a ball are on the outside of the larger circle. The players jog around in the circle and ask for a pass from a player on the outside of the circle with a ball. The jogging player stops, drops down into a passing position, and returns a one-touch pass. After each pass, the player runs through the smaller circle in the center of the larger circle before finding another player on the outside with a ball (Fig. 5.56).

Fig. 5.56

Two-Player Passing Challenge—Moderate Difficulty

Two players pass the ball one-touch back and forth through gates (two to three feet wide) that vary in depth so players are forced not only to move from one side to the other, but also up and back as they work toward the end (Fig. 5.57).

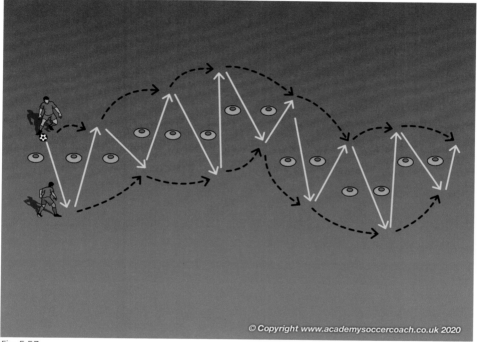

Fig. 5.57

Phase of Play	Probing
Coaching Element	#4 Probing Passing
Development Stage	II Competitive Game
Drill	"Rondo 5v3"

Learning Objective

Players will learn how to keep possession with five attacking players playing against three defenders in a restricted area.

Drill Description

Players play 5v3 in a restricted area. The team in possession scores by passing the ball seven times in a row, and the defenders score either by winning the ball and making three passes to each other or by scoring in the goal. Attacking players are limited to one or two touches.

Defenders have unlimited touches. One or two attackers can play goalkeeper when their team loses the ball (Fig. 5.58).

Fig. 5.58

Player Principle
4.3 Players need to "slide to get into supportive positions."

In the 5v3 game, the space is larger than the 5v1 game and the supportive players now have to move quickly from side to side in order to get open for a pass.

Drill Progression

1. There is a two-touch limitation.
2. There is a one-touch limitation.
3. Additional passes are needed for a point.
4. The playing area is made smaller.

Note: The playing numbers should not be changed since 5v3 is the ideal number to replicate the probing situation in an 11v11 game.

Drill Variations

- Extra point for splitting the defenders with a one-touch pass.
- Attackers earn points for either making 10 consecutive passes with unlimited touches or making 4 consecutive one-touch passes.

Coaching Interventions

Problem
Players get trapped with the ball with no options to pass.

Possible Cause #1: The players do not recognize when to play one-touch.

Practice Intervention: *Direct—Within the flow of the game, tell players at specific moments when a one-touch pass is optimal for helping them to play faster.

Possible Cause #2: The players do not recognize how to pass through seams and split the defenders.

Practice Intervention: *Explanation—Between games, explain where supportive players off the ball need to slide into positions to receive a pass. Supportive players need to "see the ball to receive a pass." *Direct—Within the game, coach players to look for seams.

Other Exercises

Rondo with Transition: 6v2—Advanced Drill

Attackers play 5v2 in a restricted area on one side of a rectangular field that has been divided into thirds. After five consecutive passes, they can pass the ball across the space to the supportive player in the other box for one point. Four players run to the opposite side to continue the game and one player remains behind as the new support player. The defenders score by winning the ball and dribbling out of the area (Fig. 5.59).

This drill mimics a game environment in which five players engage in probing before relieving the pressure by passing to the other side of the field.

Drill Variation: Add a third defender.

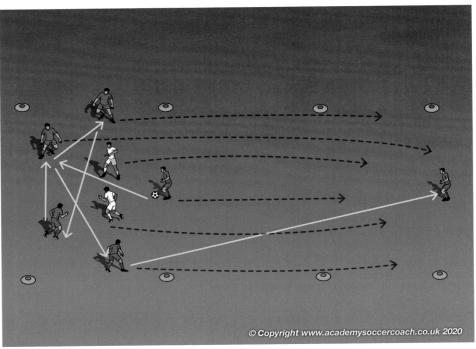

Fig. 5.59

Rondo with Sliding: 6v3—Advanced Drill

The team of six gains a point when they can make four one-touch passes within one half of the field. This requires the attacking players to slide from one side to another to create overloads so they can have more players in one area than the three defenders. After four passes, or when no more passes are possible in the half-field, then the attackers look to pass the ball to the supportive person remaining on the other half. The defenders earn a point for winning the ball and scoring on small goals at either end or making three consecutive passes (Fig. 5.60).

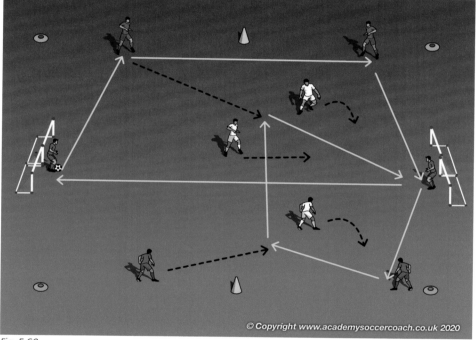

© Copyright www.academysoccercoach.co.uk 2020

Fig. 5.60

Drill Variations

- The defenders can use four players, but only three can be in one half of the field at a time. This keeps the pressure the same in each half (5v3), but makes it more challenging for the attackers to pass the ball from one side of the field to the other.
- The attackers play with seven players, with six on the outside and one in the middle acting as a playmaker.

Phase of Play	Probing
Coaching Element	#4 Probing Passing
Development Stage	III Positional Game
Drill	"Rondo End Zone Game"

Learning Objective

Players will learn how to use short, quick passing in a game-like environment to set up transitions to attack.

Drill Description

6v6

The attacking players look for opportunities to score a point by dribbling into the end zone or passing to a player running into the end zone. The attacking team can also score by making four consecutive one-touch passes in either half of the field, divided lengthwise. Defenders score by passing the ball through the small goals. The attacking team is set up in a 3-3 – three midfielders in a triangle with three forwards, and defenders are in a 4-2 (Fig. 5.61).

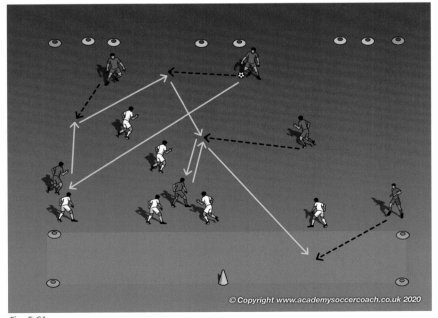

© Copyright www.academysoccercoach.co.uk 2020

Fig. 5.61

Player Principles

4.4 Players need to "shift side to side" to get numbers around the ball.

Midfielders often need reminding that they must aggressively slide from side to side to ensure they get numbers around the ball. Midfielders who hold their positions will not be able to get at least five players around the ball, which is necessary to keep possession against the defending team's midfielders and defenders. Remind them, as a reference point, that all three midfielders should be across the midline of the field when the ball is on one side of the field or the other. Show them that they are trying to create the same Rondo formation that they made in the previous practice games.

4.5 "Switch the ball when you cannot go forward."

Attackers must remember that they have the option to switch the field of play if the defense is well organized and the attackers are not able to get into the end zone. The result of getting numbers around the ball on either side of the field is that the defense will also need to commit numbers to that side of the field to defend the ball. This can leave a wide player open on the opposite side. Remind the forward away from where the ball is being played to stay appropriately wide in order to provide attackers the option of switching the field of play.

Drill Variations

- Add an extra defender.
- Change the scoring to reflect what you want to focus on. For example, attackers can only score by passing to a teammate running into the end zone and not by dribbling, or they can score just by dribbling, but not by passing.

Coaching Interventions

Problem #1

The team keeps possession but does not score.

Possible Cause: The players on the ball do not look up for attacking moments.

Practice Intervention: *Direct—Coach the players within the play when they can pass forward into the end zone after "breaking down" defenses and creating new angles and seams by quick, one-touch passing. Probing is a means to create chances to go forward and get behind the defense.

Problem #2

The team is not able to keep possession under pressure.

Possible Cause #1: The players do not support the ball with enough numbers, but instead remain rooted to their assigned positions.

Practice Intervention: *Freeze—Stop the game and move the players into the right positions so that there are enough players around the ball to keep possession. Show them how to slide into position to find the seams where they can receive the ball. *Direct—Within the flow of the game, coach players to get around the ball. At restarts, explain to players how important side-to-side movement is to keep numbers around the ball.

Possible Cause #2: The players force passes forward.

Practice Intervention: *Freeze—Stop the game and have players rehearse switching the field when direct paths to the goal are blocked. At breaks, remind players how an outlet is essential to keeping possession in the attacking half of the field. *Direct— During the run of play, the players should be reminded to switch the field when no forward pass is available.

Other Exercises

Positional Rondo Game—Advanced Drill

The attacking team plays in a 2-3-3 against the defending team, which is in a formation of 4-3 with a goalkeeper. The attacking team plays with two outside backs who support the attack when the ball is on their side. The attacking team attempts to keep possession of the ball in tight areas to create attacking chances on goal. In this game, the outside backs push up to help create numbers around the ball. The attacking team scores on goal and the defending team scores on the three goals at the halfway line. The defenders are instructed to sit back and defend in a deep position (Fig. 5.62).

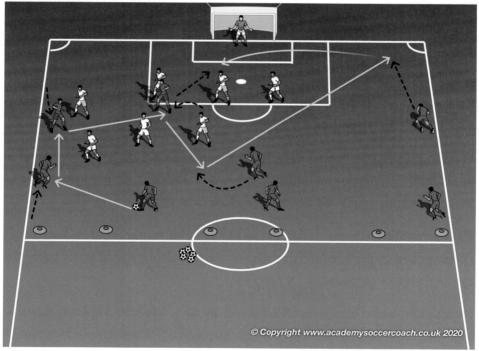

Fig. 5.62

Phase of Play	Probing
Coaching Element	#4 Probing: Passing
Development Stage	IV Standard Game
Drill	"11v11"

Learning Objective

The attacking team will learn to keep possession in the opponents' half with short, quick passing to create goal-scoring opportunities in a standard game environment.

Drill Description

4-3-3 v 4-3-3

Two teams play 11v11 on a full field. The defending team will defend deep in their defensive half and not press, so the attacking team can practice probing passing.

Player Principles

4.6 Players need to learn when after the build-up to transition to attack or to transition to probing passing.

As the team brings the ball up from the back, players around the halfway line need to decide if they can quickly transition to attack, or if they must get numbers forward to probe in the other team's half to create attacking chances.

4.7 The transition to probing must involve the "dynamic movement of the entire team as players quickly push up from the defense" into the attacking half and assume new positions relative to the ball.

The attacking team must react quickly and push up as a whole team when they transition to probing. Slow-reacting defenders who lope forward to the halfway line do not provide enough numbers (minimum five) around the ball in order to probe for goal-scoring chances against a compact and organized defense.

Coaching Interventions

Problem
The attacking team continues to lose the ball in the attacking half.

Possible Cause: The attacking team does not transition quick enough to get players around the ball to effectively probe when a direct attacking play is not possible.

Practice Intervention: *Freeze—Stop the play and show the players where they need to be as they transition from build up to probing. Outside fullbacks are typically not high enough and central midfielders typically don't shift enough to the side of the ball. *Direct—Within the run of play, coach the players to get quickly into the right positions.

Alternative Formations

9v9 Formation
3-2-3 v 3-2-3

Teams will attack in a 3-2-3, and defend in a 4-3-1. The attacking team will seek to get five players around the ball, including the outside fullback, the two center midfielders, and two forwards. One forward will stay wide for the release pass in case the probing does not create direct attacking chances. The defending team will defend with four fullbacks and three midfielders.

7v7 Formation
3-1-2 v 3-1-2

In attack, the teams will play in a 3-1-2, while the teams in defense will play in a 3-2-1. The attacking team will look to get three players around the ball—one fullback, the center midfielder and one forward—to maintain possession against the defense. The defense will have two midfielders in front of the three fullbacks. The extra forward for the attacking team will maintain width in case probing does not break down the defense.

5v5 Formation
2-1-1 v 2-1-2

The teams will attack in a 2-1-1, and defend in a 2-2. In attack, the team will position the forward, midfielder and one fullback around the ball to maintain possession against a defense that will defend in a 2-2. The attacking team's second fullback can help provide width.

COACHING ELEMENT #5 PROBING DRIBBLING

Arsenal's Mesut Özil deceptively turns away from pressure to create an attack on goal.

Phase of Play	Probing
Coaching Element	#5 Probing Dribbling
Development Stage	I Skills and Tactics
Drill	"Open Space Dribbling With Turns"

Learning Objective

Players will learn how to make deceptive and sharp turns while dribbling.

Drill Description

Each player has a ball and dribbles around the area marked with disc cones. On the coach's command, players practice different types of turning skills at each cone (Fig. 5.63).

Note: Use flat, poly spot markers if you plan to play cone tag directly afterwards.

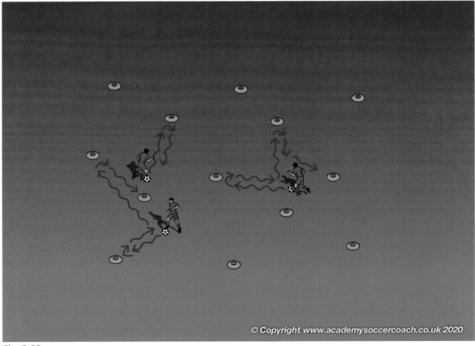

Fig. 5.63

Player Principles

5.1 The players dribble with the ball "under the body," "touching the ball every step" with the "inside and outside of the foot" and the "head up."

Dribbling in tight areas requires the player to keep the ball very close. The dribbler must be able to move the ball in any direction in order to avoid pressure and create attacking opportunities. In this probing dribbling, the ball does not go in straight lines, but goes from side to side with each touch.

5.2 The dribbler needs to "turn quickly" to create space.

The dribbler needs to turn quickly and suddenly to escape trouble and set up attacks. Predictable, slow turns will be read by the defense and not allow the dribbler to escape trouble or to create chances.

5.3 The players should "shield with a wide stance."

Players should stand sideways when shielding so both feet are between the defending player and the ball. The player on the ball leans into the defender to protect the ball and not get pushed off. The dribbler should not keep one foot on the ball because the dribbler could lose balance with physical contact. Players must keep the ball close with little touches, using the outside of the foot that is farthest from the defending player.

Skills Introduced
Dribbling

- Roll back
- Cut
- Outside-of-the-foot turn
- Cruyff turn
- Step-over
- Roll-push
- Xavi pirouette (cut-back)
- Shielding

Drill Progression

1. Players practice probing dribbling by dribbling only with the inside and outside of the foot—no straight lines—touching the ball every step in a slightly new direction, with the knee and body over the ball and the head up. Players should curve in and out of the cones and around other players within the designated area.
2. Perform the roll back on the cones—both feet.
3. Perform the cut on the cones—both feet.
4. Perform the outside-of-the-foot cut on cones—both feet.
5. Perform the Cruyff turn on cones—strong foot.
6. Perform the step-over on cones—both feet.
7. Perform the roll-push on cones—both feet.
8. Perform the Xavi pirouette (cut-back) on cones.
9. Perform shielding of the ball in one place.

Drill Variations

- Do the same drill without cones—players turn on the coach's command or when they confront another player.
- Add a change of speed after a turn for a couple of yards, with the top of the foot dribbling in a straight line. (Remind players in drills like this that they are "responsible for their safety" and need to get their heads up and pick a channel to dribble through before they dribble fast.)
- Half the players have a ball and half do not. The players without a ball move around the area and confront a player with a ball who does a turn to get away from the pressure. This variation makes it harder for the dribblers because they have to time their turns while the defending player is moving toward them. After confronting a player, the defender moves toward another dribbler to apply pressure, but without actually trying to get the ball.

Coaching Interventions

Problem

The turns are not sharp enough.

Possible Cause #1: The dribbler has the ball too far from the foot and not under the body, so the player has to reach for the ball or take extra steps to get close enough to the ball to do the turn.

Practice Intervention: *Freeze—Demonstrate to the players how to perform probing dribbling. Explain that the dribbler has to keep the ball close by touching the ball every step with the inside or outside of the foot. *Brief Drill Change—Stop the drill and shrink the space where players can dribble. If cones are on the field, have players pick out a triangle formed by a set of three cones that are a couple of yards apart from each other. By drastically shrinking the space where a player can dribble, players are forced to keep the ball closer, while utilizing the inside and outside of the foot. The small space also stops players from dribbling in straight lines. Many players have the habit of taking large touches when dribbling. Once players demonstrate the ability to keep the ball close in the much-reduced area, then let them dribble again in the larger space. *Direct—While they are dribbling, coach players to keep the ball closer and not let the ball run away from them: "As the player, you are in charge of the ball." Sometimes it appears that the ball is leading the player around. In this drill, the goal is to "have fun" and "be creative" while touching the ball as much as possible—"Don't dribble in straight lines."

Possible Cause #2: Players have poor turning technique.

Practice Intervention: *Neuromuscular Training—Ask players to perform the body positions for each skill movement prior to performing the skills in the drill. *Freeze—Stop the drill and demonstrate the correct way to perform the turn. Players should rehearse each move slowly prior to doing the turn with speed.

Competitive Games

Cone Tag—Easy Drill

Players are in pairs with one ball. One player starts with the ball and attempts to stop the ball on top of a poly spot marker for a point. The defender cannot touch the ball, but can stop the player from getting a point by stepping on the cone first. While the defender's foot is on the cone, the dribbler cannot stop the ball at that cone but must go to another cone. Play for 40 to 60 seconds and then switch so the defender has the ball and the attacker defends. The winner is the player with the most points after each player has had a chance to dribble. This game is excellent for players to practice turning in a game-like situation, since the best way to score a point is to dribble in one direction before suddenly turning and going the opposite direction after the defender has committed to stepping on a cone.

Drill Variations

- Players can steal the ball from each other. In this game, you play only one time for 40 to 60 seconds. Players score the same way by stopping the ball on a poly spot.
- Players get an extra point if they can do a certain move prior to stopping the ball on a cone. (This is a good rule to get players to attempt harder skills like the step-over.)
- Players can only do one specific turn, say, a cut, to get free from the defender. (This also encourages players to perfect harder moves.)

1v1 Shielding Game—Moderate Difficulty

Player 1 is offense, player 2 is defense, and player 3 is the bumper. Player 2, who starts on the sideline, passes the ball to player 1, who is standing inside the square. After the pass, player 2 runs into the square in order to steal the ball from player 1 and pass to player 3. Player 1 maintains possession as long as possible, using turns and shielding to keep the ball away from player 2. After the defender wins the ball and passes to player 3, or kicks the ball out of bounds, players switch positions—player 3 becomes the defender, player 2 becomes the attacker, and player 1 becomes the bumper (Fig. 5.64).

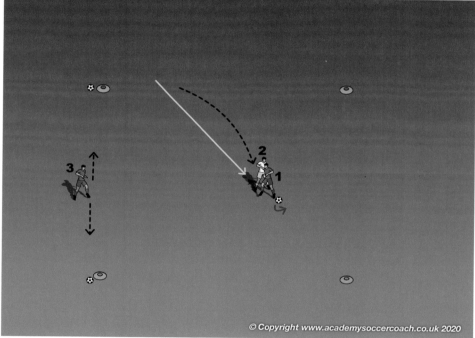

Fig. 5.64

Other Exercises

Circle Dribbling with Turns—Easy Drill

Players and their partners have one ball on the outside of a circle, with a smaller circle in the middle. Players take turns dribbling into the center of the circle, performing a turn, and dribbling back to their partners on the outside, who then repeat the drill (Fig. 5.65).

Fig. 5.65

Line Dribbling with Turns—Moderate Difficulty

Two players with one ball start at a cone facing another group of two players with a ball. At the same time, players from each side dribble to the cone, perform a turn, and dribble back to their partners, who then dribble up to the cone (Fig. 5.66).

Fig. 5.66

Drill Variation: Remove the cone and have the players turn when they meet in the center.

Phase of Play	Probing
Coaching Element	#5 Probing Dribbling
Development Stage	II Competitive Game
Drill	"3v3 + 3 Probing Dribbling Game"

Learning Objective

Players will learn how to turn under pressure to create passing opportunities.

Drill Description

3v3+3

Three players play against three players in a designated area, with three bumpers on the outside of the square who support the team with the ball. Each team tries to keep possession of the ball by passing to their teammates and the bumpers. The bumpers have two touches (or two seconds) to make a pass. The players in the box have unlimited touches. Teams score by making five to eight passes in a row, counting the passes to and from the bumpers (Fig. 5.67).

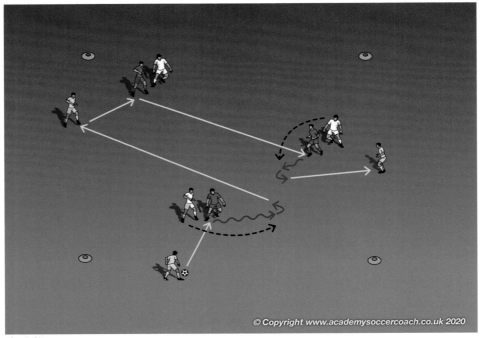

Fig. 5.67

Player Principle

5.4 Players need to "use creative turns" to elude their marker.

Because of the man-to-man marking, this drill requires players to dribble and turn away from trouble to get free to make a pass.

Drill Variations

- Don't allow players to pass directly back to the bumper who passed to them.
- Add a bonus point if the player on the ball does a specific turn to get free to make a pass, for example, a step-over.
- The number of bumpers can be reduced to make the game more difficult as players improve.
- Add a rule that the defender must stop defending the player dribbling the ball for two seconds if the dribbler is able to do a turn under pressure.
- Change the pairings so that the dribblers who are newer to turning are not man-marked by an overly aggressive and athletic defender.
- Make the space bigger so the dribblers have less pressure and more room to dribble.

Coaching Interventions

Problem

The players frequently lose the ball.

Possible Cause #1: The players on the ball do not try to turn with the ball away from pressure, but force the ball into defenders.

Practice Intervention: *Demonstrate—Between games, show the players the different turns used to create space. Have players practice a few more times to confirm they understand the technique. Perhaps focus on only one or two turns in this review to ensure that the dribblers are competent enough to do at least one move under pressure in a competitive game. *Direct—During the run of play, coach players at the appropriate time to use a turn to get away from pressure and not force the ball "through ankles."

Possible Cause #2: The player on the ball does not have enough space to turn and make a pass.

Practice Intervention: *Explain—Between games, discuss where supporting players can best support the ball without collapsing on the dribbler. When in close, high-pressure areas of the field, supporting players can slide into gaps or drop behind the ball, rather than check to the ball. It is common for players to get too close to a player who is under pressure and attempting to dribble away. Supporting players who get too close to the dribbler only drag more pressuring defenders toward the ball, making it even more difficult for the dribbler to get free of the marker. *Direct—Coach players in the game to provide the right type of support. *Drill Change—Make the field bigger.

Other Exercises

1v1 Probing Game to Three Small Goals—Moderate Difficulty

Player 3 passes to player 1, who tries to turn and pass the ball through any of the three small goals while being defended by player 2. Add a time limit to increase the speed at which the attacking player must find a passing option (Fig. 5.68).

Fig. 5.68

Drill Variations

- The dribbler can pass through the goals for one point or dribble through for two points. Also, passing or dribbling through the center goal can be worth double points.

- This drill can also be done with only two players, with the attacking player starting a yard in front of the defending player. The attacker sprints out to a ball sitting five yards away on the line and tries to turn to get free to make the pass. Several soccer balls can also be set out so the attacking player can fake to one ball but go to another. The defender can't try to win the ball until the attacking player touches it.

Phase of Play	Probing
Coaching Element	#5 Probing Dribbling
Development Stage	III Positional Game
Drill	"7v7 Probing Dribbling End Zone Game"

Learning Objective

Players will learn to use dribbling turns under pressure in a game-like situation to create attacking opportunities.

Drill Description

The attacking team plays in a 1-3-3 against the defensive team in a 4-3 formation. The attacking team scores a point by passing the ball to a player running into the end zone. The three defensive midfielders man-mark the three attacking midfielders, so there is always pressure on the ball and a need to turn away from pressure to go forward. The defending team scores on the three small goals (Fig. 5.69).

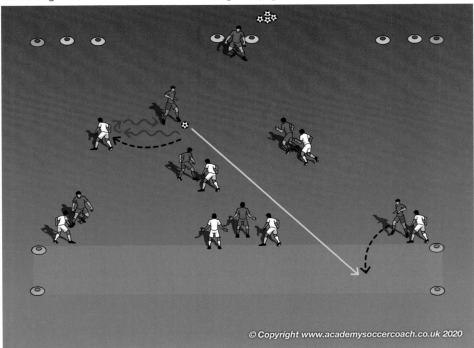

Fig. 5.69

Player Principles
5.5 Players will use turns to "create attacking opportunities."

Coaches should encourage players to trust their instincts in order to find creative ways to turn out of pressure and create attacking opportunities.

Coaching Interventions

Problem
The attacking players do not score.

Possible Cause: The attacking players are not in sync with one another.

Practice Intervention: *Freeze—Stop the play and demonstrate how players on the ball need to get their heads up quickly and look forward after making a turn in order to pass to a teammate running into the end zone. Players off the ball need to anticipate when a player could turn away from pressure and pass to them. *Direct—Within the game, coach players at the right times to turn away from pressure and look up to create attacking opportunities. *Explain—At restarts, discuss with the attacking team what needs improvement and what went well in the previous play.

Other Exercises

6v8+3 Probing Dribbling Positional Game to a Standard Goal—Advanced Drill

The attacking team plays in a 3-3 formation and scores on the large goal. The attacking team uses the three bumpers to help keep possession. The defending team in a 4-3 formation scores by passing to the same bumper players. Normal soccer rules are in effect, except that the ball restarts from a bumper player when the ball goes out of bounds (Fig. 5.70).

Fig. 5.70

Phase of Play	Probing
Coaching Element	#5 Probing Dribbling
Development Stage	IV Standard Game
Drill	"11v11"

Learning Objective

Players will learn how to use probing dribbling and surprising, creative turns to develop attacking opportunities in a game environment.

Drill Description

4-3-3 v 4-3-3

In this game, teams man-mark each other in the midfield so each team can focus on turning under pressure to create attacking opportunities.

Player Principle

5.6 Players will learn "when to pass and when to dribble and turn" in attacking situations.

Players will need to decide when to pass to a teammate in order to keep possession and when to use turns and dribble away from pressure in order to create attacking opportunities.

Hesitant players should be encouraged to try turns combined with probing dribbling to create attacking chances. The goal is to train players to have the right balance between taking chances and playing it safe.

Coaching Interventions

Problem

The teams lose the ball in attacking situations.

Possible Cause #1: The players are not transitioning well to probing passing that sets up opportunities to do probing dribbling.

Practice Intervention: *Freeze—Stop the game to rehearse the movement required to get numbers around the ball in the opposition's half when a direct attack on goal is not possible. Demonstrate when a player would use a deceptive turn to create an attack. *Direct—Encourage players during the game to push forward into supportive positions around the ball and slide from side to side to provide support.

Possible Cause #2: The players on the ball make the wrong choices when to turn and when to pass.

Practice Intervention: *Direct—Coach players in the game when to perform turns to create attacking opportunities to score and when to pass to keep possession. Some players might need encouragement to perform turns, while others might need reminders to pass more, and turn less.

Alternative Formations

9v9 Formation
3-2-3 v 3-2-3

Both teams man-mark in the midfield. Midfielders from both teams focus on probing dribbling to free themselves from their defenders in order to make space for attacking opportunities.

7v7 Formation
2-3-1 v 2-3-1

The midfield will line up in a triangle to mirror their positions when they play 11v11.

5v5 Formation
1-2-1 v 1-2-1

Both teams man-mark in the midfield.

Skills for Probing Dribbling

Step-Over

In a game environment, the step-over can be a deceptive way to fake an intention to dribble one way with a defender on one's back before dribbling in the opposite direction. The initial step forward should persuade the defender to shift in that direction, leaving room to turn around and go in the opposite direction.

1 Soccer Position

"Stand with your feet facing forward, knees softly bent, feet just wider than shoulder width, engaged at the core" (Fig. 3.1, *a* and *b*).

2 Skill

a) "Take the right foot and step forward around the outside of the ball so the right foot ends up in front of the left planting foot, still facing straight ahead" (Fig. 5.70*a*).

Fig. 5.70a

"Now, turn back to your right side by pivoting on the forward right foot so the back left foot swings around and back toward the ball. Take the ball with the inside of the left foot going in the opposite direction to the one you were initially facing" (Fig. 5.70*b*).

Fig. 5.70b

b) "Dribble around in the area and perform step-overs so you end up dribbling in the opposite direction."

c) "Perform the first step around the ball as fast as possible, as if you are about to quickly run forward, before decisively turning back in the other direction."

Outside-of-the-Foot Turn

The outside-of-the foot turn allows a player to quickly and deceptively change directions.

1 Soccer Position

"Stand with your feet facing forward, knees softly bent, feet just wider than shoulder width, engaged at the core" (Figs. 3.1, *a* and *b*).

2 Open Skill Position

"Reach straight forward with your cutting foot and point your toe outward and perpendicular to the planting foot, and place the outside of your foot on the far side of the ball, angled back toward the body ." (Fig. 5.71)

Fig. 5.71

3 Skill

a) "The angled part of the cutting foot should come straight down on the far side of the ball so it strikes the ball and pushes it in the opposite direction from the one you're facing."

b) "Dribble around and cut the ball sharply."

c) "After making the cut, dribble quickly away in the new direction."

Cruyff Turn

The Cruyff turn can get a defender to lunge at the ball before the turn takes the dribbler in the opposite direction.

1 Soccer Position

"Stand with your feet facing forward, knees softly bent, feet just wider than shoulder width, engaged at the core" (Figs. 3.1, *a* and *b*).

2 Grounded Skill Position

"Place your foot behind the ball with your toe pointing inward and resting on the ground. This foot will be used to cut the ball. The cutting foot is perpendicular to the planting foot, with the heel of the cutting foot slightly off the ground. Your knees almost touch each other as your feet form a right angle and pinch inwards" (Fig. 5.72*a*).

Fig. 5.72a

3 Open Skill Position

"Lift the cutting foot into the air holding it behind the ball."

4 Skill

a) "Flick the ball behind you with your cutting foot so the ball goes past your planting foot and directly behind you. Pivot around on your planting foot away from the ball and face the opposite direction, where the ball is waiting for your next play" (Fig. 5.72b).

Fig. 5.72b

b) "Dribble around the area and perform quick Cruyff turns so that you end up dribbling in the opposite direction."

c) "Dribble around and perform the Cruyff turn with the fake-shot arm movement. While you step with your left planting foot toward the ball, lift your left arm in the air at the same time, to maintain balance as you pull back your right leg as if preparing to kick the ball with power. Left arm and left foot are synchronized moving forward at the same time. Bring the right foot forward as if to kick the ball, but instead pivot the right foot inward and quickly perform the Cruyff turn" (Fig. 5.72c).

d) "After performing the Cruyff turn with the fake-shot arm movement, dribble off quickly in the new direction."

Fig. 5.72c

Xavi Pirouette Turn (Cut-Back)

As can be seen in figure 5.73, the player on the ball can use this turn to lure the defending player out of position by 1) exposing the ball, 2) moving the ball just out of reach with a small touch, and 3) turning all the way around and proceeding to dribble where the defender was originally standing and blocking the way forward.

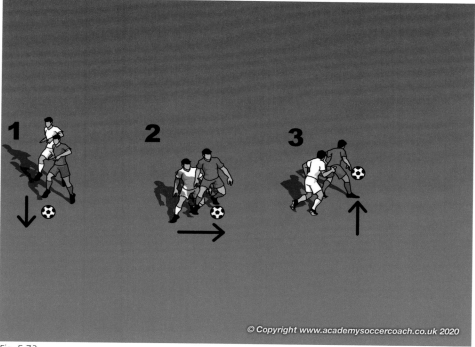

Fig. 5.73

1 Soccer Position

"Stand with your feet facing forward, knees softly bent, feet just wider than shoulder width, engaged at the core" (Fig. 3.1, *a* and *b*).

2 Skill

a) "Use the inside of the right foot to tap the ball directly ahead about a foot" (Fig. 5.74*a*).

Fig. 5.74a

"Pivot left on the left planting foot and use the inside of the right foot to tap the ball to the left in front of your body" (Fig. 5.74b).

Fig. 5.74b

"Pivot again to the left and use the inside of the right foot to tap the ball back to your left side, so you are facing the opposite direction from the way you started" (Fig. 5.74c).

Fig. 5.74c

b) "Dribble around and perform the Xavi pirouette turn so you end up dribbling in the opposite direction after the turn."

c) "Dribble quickly in the new direction after the Xavi pirouette turn."

Roll-Push Turn

This turn can be useful in tight areas. The dribbler can pull the ball away from an opponent reaching for the ball and can quickly take the ball at a 90-degree angle away from pressure.

1 Soccer Position

"Stand with your feet facing forward, knees softly bent, feet just wider than shoulder width, engaged at the core" (Figs. 3.1, *a* and *b*).

2 Skill

a) "Place the sole of your right foot on top of the ball and roll the ball toward you, as in a roll back" (Fig. 5.75*a*).

Fig. 5.75a

"At the same time as you roll the ball back toward you, as if to do a roll back, hop up with the left foot and pivot 90 degrees to the right. You are now facing in the new direction at a right angle to where you started" (Fig. 5.75b).

Fig. 5.75b

"Without letting the right foot touch the ground after the roll back, touch the ball in the new direction with the inside of the right foot" (Fig. 5.75c).

Fig. 5.75c

b) "Dribble around and quickly and smoothly perform the roll-push so you end up dribbling at a right angle to the direction you were originally facing."

c) "Dribble with increased speed after performing the roll-push."

COACHING ELEMENT #6 ATTACKING DRIBBLING

Brazil's Marta dribbles at the defender.

Phase of Play	Attacking
Coaching Element	#6 Attacking Dribbling
Development Stage	I Skills and Tactics
Drill	"Attacking Dribbling Moves at Cones in Straight Lines"

Learning Objective

Players will learn attacking dribbling moves.

Drill Description

Two players dribble toward the center cone at the same time, perform attacking moves at the cone, and proceed to the opposite side (Fig. 5.76).

Fig. 5.76

Player Principle

6.1 "Make the move early enough."

It is important that players make the move far enough in front of the cone so they do not run into it. Each move has its space requirements. For example, the scissors move can require more space in front of the cone than a fake left, go right.

Skills Introduced

Dribbling

- Top-of-the-foot dribbling
- Change of speed
- Fake left, go right
- Scissors
- Ronaldo Chop
- Inside-outside

Shooting

- Instep shot

Drill Progression

1. Players dribble at medium speed to the opposite side with the top of the feet, without changing speed or completing a move. Each player should dribble to the right of the center cone.
2. Players dribble at medium speed to the right of the center cone and then accelerate straight with the ball after they pass the cone, without making an attacking move.
3. Players dribble straight at the center cone, do an attacking move, and accelerate to the opposite side. Intending to meet at the center cone at the same time, both players will go to their right after the move so they avoid hitting each other.
4. Players make the same moves to their left.

Drill Variations

- Remove the cone so players dribble directly at each other and have to do the move before they meet. This makes the drill harder, as timing is added.
- Remove the cone, and have only one player dribble at a time, performing the drill in the open space. This makes the drill easier.

Coaching Interventions

Problem

The players dribble into the center cone while trying to do the move.

Possible Cause #1: The players dribble the ball too far in front of themselves.

Practice Intervention: *Freeze—Demonstrate how to strike the ball with the instep. Even when players speed up, they should have the ball under full control and touch the ball with each step. *Direct—While the players are doing the drill, coach them to dribble with the ball closer—"toe down, head up"—using their insteps before making the attacking move.

Possible Cause #2: The players do not know how to do 1v1 moves.

Practice Intervention: *Neuromuscular training—Break the skills down into specific postures and movements for players to practice prior to doing them in the drill. Have players practice the 1v1 moves while standing in one spot, before they perform them while moving.

Competitive Games

1v1 Attacking Dribbling Game to End Zones—Easy Drill

Players on one side pass the ball to the opposite side and become the defenders. The player who receives the ball attempts to dribble around the defending player and into the end zone. After the attacker scores or the defender wins the ball, the players switch roles. Players keep track of how many points they get in the time allotted. Multiple pairings play at once (Fig. 5.77).

Note: Remind players that they are in charge of their safety. With so many players in one area, each player needs to keep the head up to avoid colliding with another.

Fig. 5.77

1v1 Attacking Dribbling Through a Defended Zone—Moderate Difficulty

Player 1 attempts to dribble through the rectangular zone guarded by the defender, who cannot leave the zone. If the attacker dribbles through the zone, the dribbler gets a point. If the defender wins the ball, then the attacker switches with the defender and the defender becomes the attacker (Fig. 5.78).

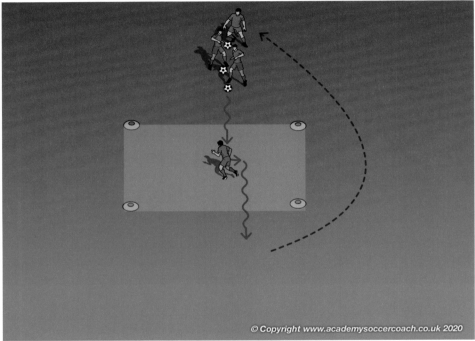

Fig. 5.78

Other Exercises

Attacking Dribbling at Cones in an Open Area—Easy Drill

Each player has a ball and dribbles in the area with randomly placed cones. Players perform attacking moves on cones, accelerating after each move into an open space. This drill allows everybody to dribble at once (Fig. 5.79).

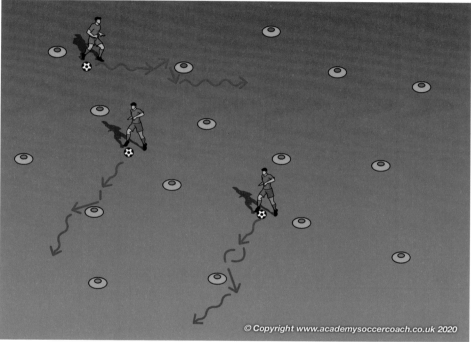

Fig. 5.79

Attacking Dribbling Through Random Cones—Moderate Difficulty

Players, each with a ball, line up on one side of the field and, practicing various moves, dribble across the field through the area of dense, randomly placed cones about a yard apart. Aim for, say, three to five moves each time up and back. On the coach's command, one group goes at a time. When one group is halfway across, the next group starts dribbling. The first group can start back across once the last group has made it through the cones to the opposite side (Fig. 5.80).

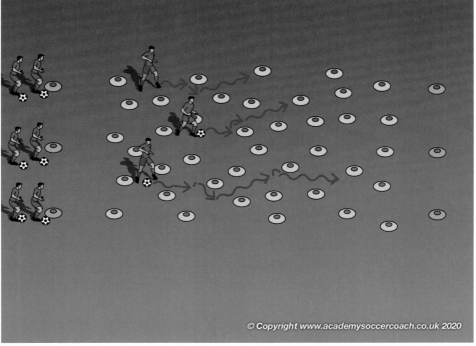

© Copyright www.academysoccercoach.co.uk 2020

Fig. 5.80

Attacking Dribbling Through Space—Moderate Difficulty

Players, each with a ball, are in lines on one side of the field. Each group dribbles across the field, which is divided into three sections. In the first section, the players dribble at medium speed with the top of the foot. In the middle section, players do an attacking dribbling move four to six times without accelerating after the move. In the third section, players do the move two times and accelerate after each move. The first group waits at the other side for the next groups to finish before returning (Fig. 5.81).

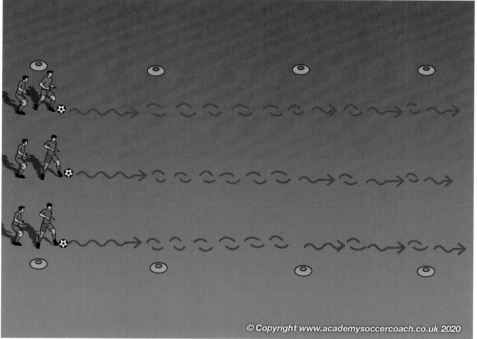

Fig. 5.81

Sequential Attacking Cone Dribbling—Advanced Drill

Players with a ball stand behind a gate, as shown in the diagram. Players dribble up one set of cones, then back down the next set of cones, repeating up and back until they have completed all the cone drills. Once they finish the last drill, the players dribble back to their beginning gate. Players will do a different move or style of dribbling at each set of cones, alternating between performing dribble moves and speed dribbling. Players will have three sets of prescribed drills that they will do two or three times each (Fig. 5.82).

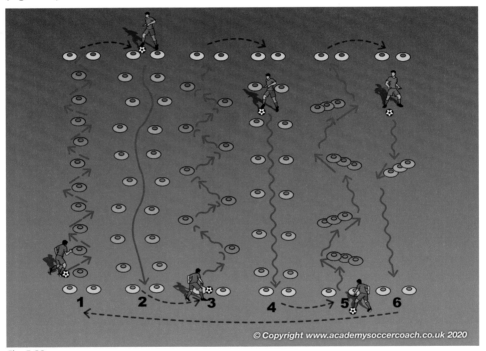

Fig. 5.82

Here is an example of how to organize three sets of dribbling sequences. Players should be evenly spread out behind the outside gates when they start.

First Round

1. Dribble through cones with just the right foot—two touches inside and two touches outside between cones. *No straddling cones, i.e., both feet must go through each gate.
2. Dribble back as fast as possible within the gates, using the inside and outside of the foot to navigate the curved path.
3. Dribble up the cones, performing a cut at each cone.
4. Dribble back through the gates in a straight line as fast as possible.
5. Dribble up through the cones doing a fake left, go right at each cone without acceleration.
6. Dribble back performing one fake left, go right at the three cones, followed by acceleration. Dribble back to the beginning along the side.

Second Round

1. Dribble with just the left foot through cones, two touches inside and two touches outside, through each opening.
2. Dribble back as fast as possible within the gates, using only the left foot.
3. Dribble up the cones, performing a scissors at the inside of each cone.
4. Dribble back through the gates in a straight line with the left foot.
5. Dribble up through the cones, performing an inside-outside move without acceleration.
6. Dribble back, performing a scissors at the three cones followed by acceleration. Dribble back to the beginning along the side.

Third Round

1. Dribble with just the outside of the left and right feet—always touching the ball two times between cones. *Note: Players must shuffle their feet quickly left and right to get the body past the ball in order to line up the next outside-of-the-foot touch. Players should not reach the foot across the body for the ball.
2. Dribble back as fast as possible.
3. Dribble up and cut with the outside of the foot at each cone. Players should reach for the ball and snap the ball in the new direction.
4. Dribble back through the cones as fast as possible.
5. Dribble up through the cones, doing a scissors at each cone without acceleration.
6. Dribble back, doing a double scissors at the three cones followed by acceleration. Dribble back to the beginning along the side.

Sequential Dribbling Ending with a Shot on Goal—Easy Drill

Players dribble through cones in various ways to practice attacking moves, and then end with a shot on a standard-size goal. Alternate the dribbling moves every few minutes.

Phase of Play	Attacking
Coaching Element	#6 Attacking Dribbling
Development Stage	II Competitive Game
Drill	"2v2 With End Zones"

Learning Objective

Players will improve their ability to get past a defender utilizing an attacking dribble move.

Drill Description

2v2

Two teams of two play against one another with the goal of dribbling the ball into the end zone (Fig. 5.83).

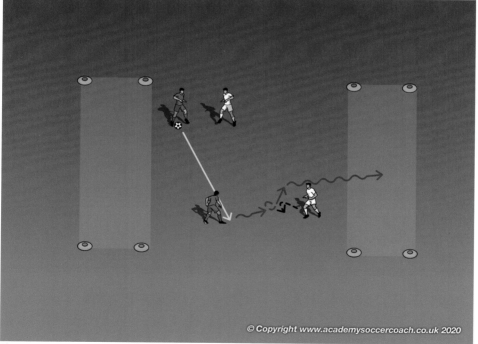

Fig. 5.83

225

Player Principles

6.2 "Dribble straight at the defender" in order to "commit and engage the defender."

When attackers can get defenders to commit to the ball by dribbling at them, defenders are forced to engage or risk being easily beaten. The attacker now can use a fake to get the defender to move in one direction while the attacker dribbles past.

When players dribble in a straight direction at a fast pace, it is important to use the top of the foot so they do not have to look down after each touch and will always know the ball is straight in front of them. Dribbling with the inside and outside of the foot requires more looking at the ball since it will be moving at different angles. In open space, the player's head needs to be up as much as possible to survey the field and know when the defender has been engaged.

6.3 "Know when to pass and when to dribble."

Players on the ball should be coached about when they should dribble past an opponent and when they should pass the ball off to a teammate. One cue to dribble around an opponent is that the dribbler is challenged by one player, not two. The dribbler will have a better chance going past the defender if the dribbler is already moving at moderate speed. This allows the dribbler to accelerate to top speed faster after making the move. Standing still when pressed by a defender is a reason to pass to a teammate.

Drill Variations

- The field can be made wider to make the game easier and narrower to make the game harder.
- More players can be added to make it harder to dribble.

Coaching Interventions

Problem #1

The players do not dribble around the defenders.

Possible Cause: The players do not dribble at defenders at moderate speed before making the 1v1 move.

Practice Intervention: *Demonstrate—Between games, show players that the best way to dribble around a defender is to attack them at speed. *Drill Change—Make the field wider so it is easier to dribble around opponents. The coach can also change the teams so that players are not overmatched.

Problem #2

The player dribbling continues to be double-teamed, making it too difficult to dribble into the end zone.

Possible Cause #1: The supporting player is too close to the dribbler, taking away dribbling space and unintentionally dragging the second defender close to the dribbler.

Practice Intervention: *Demonstrate—Between games, show the supporting players where to position themselves to give the dribbler space to dribble and decrease the pressure from the second defender. The supportive player needs to be in a good position to receive a pass without blocking the player who is dribbling. *Direct—Within the game, coach the supportive player to give the dribbler space.

Possible Cause #2: The dribbler waits too long to engage and make a move against the defender, allowing the second defender time to slide over and help.

Practice Intervention: *Direct—Within the game, coach the player who is dribbling about when to commit the defender and attempt to get around the opponent.

Other Exercises

1v1 to Goal—Moderate Difficulty

The attacker dribbles at the defender to try and score on the goal. The defender should not move toward the ball until the attacker starts dribbling. Play ends when the ball is scored or kicked out of play. Attacker and defender switch after each play (Fig. 5.84).

Fig. 5.84

Drill Variation: Two players trying to score a goal attack two defenders.

1v1 to Goal with Agility—Moderate Difficulty

Players run through an obstacle course with agility challenges before the ball is passed to the attacking player, who then attempts to dribble around the defender and score on the goal. The agility course should be set up so that the attacking players have time to run through the cones, receive the ball, and turn before being put under pressure. This is a good drill to improve fitness, speed, and attacking dribbling (Fig. 5.85).

Fig. 5.85

Phase of Play	Attacking
Coaching Element	#6 Attacking Dribbling
Development Stage	III Positional Game
Drill	"5v4 End Zone Game"

Learning Objective

Players will improve their ability to dribble past opponents under game-like conditions.

Drill Description

The attacking team scores by dribbling into the end zone in a 2-3 formation against a defense in a 3-1 formation. Defenders score by winning the ball and passing it through the small goals (Fig. 5.86).

Fig. 5.86

Player Principle

6.4 The attacking team should "find players who are 1v1."

Players on the attacking team should look for opportunities to set their teammates up to go 1v1 against an opponent.

Coaching Interventions

Problem

The attacking team does not create good 1v1 dribbling opportunities to score.

Possible Cause: The attacking team makes the wrong choices about when to attempt dribbling over the end zone.

Practice Intervention: *Freeze—Stop the game and explain that the attacking team should seek to create opportunities for players who have good attacking options to dribble into the end zone, such as passing to players away from pressure in wide areas. *Explain—During the restarts, review decisions made by attackers in the previous play. *Drill Change—Make the field wider.

Other Exercise

6v6 Positional Attacking Dribbling Game to a Standard Goal—Advanced Drill

The attacking team plays in a 3-3 formation and scores on goal. The defending team is in a 3-2 formation and scores by dribbling over the line 10 yards in from the halfway line. Add a fourth defender once the attackers appear to need more of a challenge (Fig. 5.87).

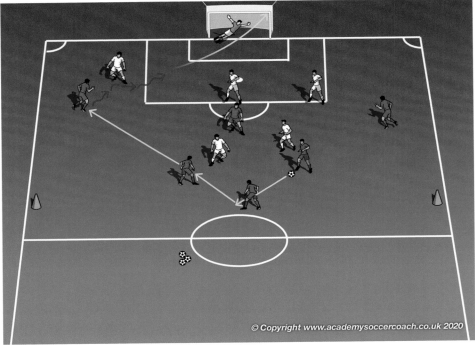

Fig. 5.87

Phase of Play	Attacking
Coaching Element	#6 Attacking Dribbling
Development Stage	IV Standard Game
Drill	"11v11"

Learning Objective

Players will improve their ability to dribble 1v1 to set up goal-scoring chances in a standard game.

Drill Description

4-3-3 v 4-3-3

In this game, forwards are expected to demonstrate how 1v1 dribbling can exploit opportunities to score.

Playing Principle

6.5 Players need to "take players on in the right areas of the field."

Coaching Interventions

Problem

The attacking players do not create opportunities to score on goal.

Possible Cause: The attacking players dribble in the wrong areas, at the wrong time, or at the wrong angles.

Practice Intervention: *Freeze—Stop the game and show the players where and when they need to dribble 1v1 to create shots on goal transitioning from build-up and probing. A larger field with more players poses spatial and timing issues that were not present in the previous drills. Wide areas of the field, where there is more space, are often good places to dribble 1v1. *Direct—Coach within the game about how players can exploit defenses with dribbling by taking advantage of 1v1 situations. *Drill Change—Move players around to create advantageous matchups for the attackers.

Alternative Formations

9v9 Formation
3-2-3 v 3-2-3

Teams play in the same formation and look for ways for the three forwards to create goal-scoring chances through 1v1 dribbling.

7v7 Formation
2-3-1 v 2-3-1

Teams create goal-scoring chances by pushing up outside midfielders into attack.

5v5 Formation
2-2 v 2-2

Teams create goal-scoring chances through the 1v1 dribbling of the two forwards.

Skills for Attacking Dribbling

Top-of-the-Foot Dribbling

Dribbling moves generally include both change of direction and change of speed. However, the simplest dribbling move is to change speed and accelerate forward past the defender.

1 Soccer Position

"Stand with your feet facing forward, knees softly bent, feet just wider than shoulder width, engaged at the core" (Figs. 3.1, *a* and *b*).

2 Grounded Skill Position

"Point your toe down with the instep facing forward. Your toe is slightly pointed inward and resting on the ground" (Fig 5.88*a*).

Fig. 5.88a

3 Open Skill Position

"Lift your foot slightly off the ground while keeping the foot pointed straight down so the foot makes a flat surface toward the ball with the toe angled slightly inward."

4 Skill

a) "Touch the ball with every step while dribbling in a straight line with a pointed, slightly inward foot and a firm ankle. Lift your head up after every touch" (Fig. 5.88b).

Fig. 5.88b

b) "Dribble at medium speed with the top of your foot."

c) "Dribble at medium speed and then accelerate to top speed while still touching the ball with every step."

Fake Left, Go Right

The key to this move is bending the knees while dropping the left shoulder as if to run left, and then taking the ball with the outside of the right foot to go toward the right.

1 Soccer Position

"Stand with your feet facing forward, knees softly bent, feet just wider than shoulder width, engaged at the core" (Figs. 3.1, *a* and *b*).

2 Grounded Skill Position

"Point your right foot inward toward the left standing foot, which faces straight forward. Your feet should make a 45-degree angle" (Fig. 5.89*a*).

Fig. 5.89a

"With your feet in this 45-degree angle, drop your left elbow toward the left knee, which creates the fake to the left. This position makes it looks like you are about to run left" (Fig. 5.89b).

Fig. 5.89b

3 Open Skill Position

a) "Lift the right, angled foot slightly off the ground and hold it in the air" (Fig. 5.89c).

Fig. 5.89c

238

"Now, with the right foot off the ground and still at an angle, leap forward at a 45-degree angle from your left foot onto your right foot" (Fig. 5.89d).

Fig. 5.89d

b) "Without a ball, run at medium speed straight at the cone and when you get in front of the cone, put all your weight on your left foot, angle the right foot inward while it is in the air, and leap forward onto your right foot at a 45-degree angle. Accelerate past the cone after making the move" (Fig. 5.89e).

Fig. 5.89e

4 Skill

"Dribble at the cone at medium speed and fake left and go right—striking the ball with the outside of the foot to take the ball at an angle past the cone. After making the move, accelerate with top of the foot dribbling" (Fig. 5.89f).

Fig. 5.89f

Cut

The cut is a dynamic move to change directions and get past an opponent. Players can dribble in one direction to lure the defender one way before quickly cutting the ball back in the opposite direction.

1 Soccer Position

"Stand with your feet facing forward, knees softly bent, feet just wider than shoulder width, engaged at the core" (Figs. 3.1, *a* and *b*).

2 Grounded Skill Position

"Keeping your left foot facing straight forward, extend your right foot out to the side and jab the toe straight into the ground with the heel straight up in the air. The right instep is turned and facing the planting leg. Both knees are deeply bent" (Fig. 5.90*a*).

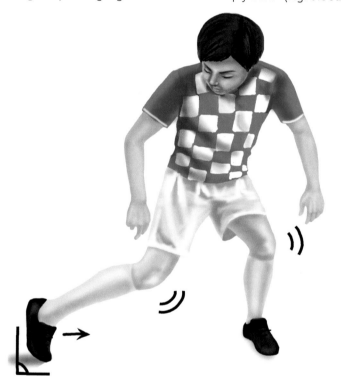

Fig. 5.90a

3 Skill

a) "Place the ball a few feet in front of you. Using the cutting technique, reach out beyond the still ball with the instep and jab down on the ball from above with both knees bent and the heel straight in the air. The left foot will pivot as you cut the ball back. If you started off facing north, then after the cut you should be facing south" (Fig. 5.90b).

Fig. 5.90b

b) "Dribble around and perform the cut."

c) "After the cut, accelerate in the new direction."

Troubleshooting

*The ball is cut back into the planting foot.

"The key to creating a sharp cut is to make sure the planting foot does not get in the way. The last step prior to making the cut should bring the planting foot just wide of the ball so there is a space, or channel, where the ball can roll in the opposite direction. You cannot cut the ball back if the planting foot is directly behind the ball."

Scissors

The scissors move is a more complex fake left, go right move. The foot going around the ball makes it seem as if you are about to go in that direction—leading the defender to shift to one side. The scissors move needs to be initiated earlier than most moves since it takes a bit of time for the foot to go all the way around the ball.

1 Soccer Position

"Stand with your feet facing forward, knees softly bent, feet just wider than shoulder width, engaged at the core" (Figs. 3.1, *a* and *b*).

2 Open Skill Position

a) "Standing directly behind the ball, move your right foot clockwise around the ball and then return the foot to the same position where it started. Now, move the left foot counterclockwise around the ball and return it to the same spot. As the foot moves around the ball, it should stay as close to the ball as possible without touching it" (Fig. 5.91, *a* and *b*).

Fig. 5.91, a and b

b) "Between the right and left scissors moves, now add several quick steps while standing in one place."

3 Skill

a) "Dribble around and perform a left scissors and then take the ball to the right with the outside of the right foot. Perform a right scissors and then take the ball to the left with the outside of the left foot" (Fig. 5.91c).

Fig. 5.91c

b) "Make the scissors move and accelerate."

c) "Perform a double scissors (left and right scissors right after each other) before taking the ball with the outside of the foot and accelerating."

Ronaldo Chop

The Ronaldo Chop is useful for wide players who want to turn inward toward the goal in a surprise move. The ball starts on one side of the player but ends up pushed out to the other side. It takes a strong crisscross movement to have the ball go a yard or so off to the side of the player.

1 Soccer Position

"Stand with your feet facing forward, knees softly bent, feet just wider than shoulder width, engaged at the core" (Figs. 3.1, *a* and *b*).

2 Open Skill Position

a) "Jump up and move the left foot forward and the right foot back, landing in a straddle position" (Fig. 5.92*a*).

Fig. 5.92a

b) "Return to the soccer position. Jump up and push the left foot forward and right foot back, but this time crisscross your legs in the air so the left leg goes up and to the right and the right leg goes back and to the left" (Fig. 5.92, *b* and *c*).

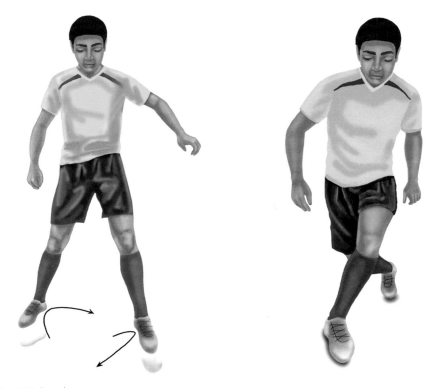

Fig. 5.92, b and c

3 Skill

a) "Stand in a soccer position with the ball between your legs. Jump and crisscross your legs so that the right leg, which is behind you, flicks the ball to your left side, behind your left leg" (Fig. 5.92*d*).

Fig. 5.92d

b) "Dribble around and practice the Ronaldo Chop, making sure the ball shoots a yard or more out to the left."

c) "Perform the Ronaldo Chop and then accelerate in the new direction."

Inside-Outside

The inside-outside should be done very quickly. The first touch moves the defender to the side, and the second touch takes the ball back past the defender. The foot should not touch the ground between the inside and outside touches. The inside-outside could be considered a stationary move, as it can also be effective when the player on the ball is not dribbling forward but is at a standstill in front of the defender.

1 Soccer Position

"Stand with your feet facing forward, knees softly bent, feet just wider than shoulder width, engaged at the core" (Figs. 3.1, *a* and *b*).

2 Skill

a) "With your weight on the left foot, hop to the left and tap the ball across your body to your left with the inside of the right foot" (Fig. 5.93*a*).

Fig. 5.93a

"Without letting the right foot touch the ground, bring the right foot quickly around to the opposite side of the ball" (Fig. 5.93b).

Fig. 5.93b

"With the outside of the right foot, take the ball forward to your right at a 45-degree angle" (Fig. 5.93c).

Fig. 5.93c

b) "Dribble around and perform the inside-outside at a cone."

c) "Accelerate after making the inside-outside move."

Instep Shot

The instep shot is the most powerful way to shoot a soccer ball. There are variations on the instep shot whereby the toe is pushed out wider and the ball is struck more with the center of the instep, but that technique is often best for free kicks when the ball is still and lots of up and down movement is required to get over a wall. When shooting from the side of the goal, the instep should wrap around the ball to get the necessary curl on the ball to evade the goalkeeper. I recommended that the "pure" instep be taught first, before the variations are introduced. Most goal scorers will utilize this pure instep when shooting off the dribble directly at goal. The "instep" shot—sometimes also called a "laces shot"—is actually a misnomer, causing potential problems when players want to learn this technique. In reality, the instep is not used to strike the ball but, instead, the top of the big toe knuckle lower down on the foot.

Since there are so many components to correct instep shooting form, neuromuscular training is first performed with players sitting on the ground. Once the proper instep form and lower leg snap are established with sitting drills, then the player stands up and learns to retain the correct foot position and snapping form while also moving the full leg in a swing. Be patient because players' habits can be slow to change.

1 "Sitting" Grounded Skill Position

The ankle stretch is a good way to assess which team members have poor ankle mobility and might have trouble later during practice with this shooting technique. The foot will need to have full mobility to strike the ball with this type of shot. This stretch also helps teach players the proper positioning of the foot.

a) "Sit on the ground and put both feet straight out in front of you so your heels are only a few inches apart and your full foot is touching the ground—heel, sole and toes all touching the ground at once. Your knees are bent at right angles" (Fig. 5.94a).

Fig. 5.94a

b) "Now, while keeping your feet flat on the ground and in one spot, scoot back a few inches. You should feel a good stretch in the top of your ankles" (Fig. 5.94*b*).

Fig. 5.94b

Troubleshooting

*The feet are not flat.

"Adjust where you are sitting so your feet can be flat."

Note: Ask the players about any history of ankle injuries or ankle soreness that can be limiting ankle mobility. Some players might need physical therapy to improve ankle mobility and strength to perform this instep shot properly.

2 "Sitting" Open Skill Position

The goal of this drill is for the player to learn how to move the lower leg and foot up and down while 1) keeping the ankle firm in the instep shooting position and 2) keeping the kicking knee level with the planting knee by not lifting or moving the hip. In an instep shot, most of the power is generated from the lower leg snapping below the knee and less from the swing of the leg from the hip.

a) "With your ankles stretched and feet flat on the ground, now lift your kicking foot in the air without lifting your toe or lifting your knee. Hold your flat foot knee-high, keeping the ankle firm" (Fig. 5.94c).

Fig. 5.94c

b) "Now repeatedly and more quickly raise and lower your foot without letting your toe or knee lift in the air, while keeping the ankle firm and foot flat."

Troubleshooting

*The kicking knee moves upward when the foot lifts up.

"Place your hand on your kicking knee so it does not move up in the air when you lift your foot."

*The toe comes up when the foot lifts up.

"Return the kicking foot to the ground so the kicking foot is forced into the instep-shooting position again. Lift again slowly. Keep practicing."

*The foot shakes and won't stay still.

"Be patient and keep trying, it will settle down."

3 "Sitting" Skill

The goal of this drill is to have the players learn to keep their feet flat with a firm ankle—keeping their knees and toes from going up—while striking the ball. The ball should not have any spin and should go straight up to about head height.

This is a common drill to teach where the ball should strike on the instep while shooting. However, it is important to keep in mind that the point of this drill is not about finding the right place on the instep to strike the ball. To do this drill, players will use the middle of the instep rather than the lower part of the instep. Some coaches believe that the middle of the instep is where players should strike the ball, but in order to do so, the toe has to be pushed to the side and heel lowered, making the instep shot look like a chip, because the foot will now be more under than over the ball. So, in this drill, do not linger any longer than needed to have players demonstrate that they can strike a ball with a firm ankle. You don't want to reinforce the wrong place on the instep to strike the ball.

a) "While sitting, reach forward holding the ball with both hands over your kicking foot. Now kick the ball while holding it in your hands. Don't let go of the ball."

b) "From the sitting position, I want you to kick the ball out of your hands straight up into the air without spin, to about head height" (Fig. 5.94d).

c) "See how many consecutive kicks ('juggles') you can do from the sitting position without the ball spinning."

Fig. 5.94d

d) "From a sitting position, I want you to kick the ball out of your hands straight into the air without spin, then stand up and catch the ball before it bounces."

Note: This is a fun challenge for players, who will need to demonstrate agility and good kicking form.

Troubleshooting

*The ball hits the player on the nose.

"The toe is pointed up, so place your foot back on the ground as a reminder of how the foot needs to be flat when striking the ball."

*The ball spins off to the outside.

"Make sure to keep your foot straight. Do not let your toe turn inward, since this creates the outside spin on the ball."

4 Soccer Position

Note: Players should now be standing.

"Stand with your feet facing forward, knees softly bent, feet just wider than shoulder width, engaged at the core" (Figs. 3.1, *a* and *b*).

5 Grounded Skill Position

There is a lot to get right at this point of the drills, so don't rush. You will need to remind players to angle their knees in slightly to get the instep facing forward. The ankle should be firm, the front of the foot facing straight ahead, and the body crunched over the kicking foot.

"Point the kicking foot straight down with your toe touching the ground, a bit more than one stretched hand-width away from your planting foot. The kicking toe should be even with the toe of the planting foot. Crunch at the core, so your body is over the kicking foot with both knees slightly bent. Your kicking knee is turned slightly inward so the front of your instep is facing straight ahead" (Fig. 5.94e).

Fig. 5.94e

6 Open Skill Position

a) "Lift your kicking foot and hold it in the air in the shooting position" (Fig. 5.94*f*).

Fig. 5.94f

b) "With your shooting foot in the air, swing just the lower leg, as if striking a ball. Make sure to follow through with the swing so the kicking leg extends forward. Keep your ankle firm. The toe of the kicking foot should swing just above the ground. Do several swings in a row without putting your kicking foot back down on the ground" (Fig. 5.94*g*).

Fig. 5.94g

c) "Swing the leg faster, really snap the lower leg through the imaginary ball."

d) "While standing in the same place, take quick, small steps in between each leg swing."

7 Skill

a) "Strike the ball back and forth with your partner (5 to 10 yards apart) using the instep shooting form. The lower end of the foot, the 'top of the big toe knuckle,' should be used to strike the ball—not the actual instep, which is higher up in the center of the foot. The ball should pop off your foot with a solid thud. Players should trap the ball before striking the stationary ball back to their partners" (Fig. 5.94*h*).

Fig. 5.94h

Troubleshooting

*The ball is struck weakly—no thud, more of a flub.

"Make sure your ankle is firm and you snap from the knee."

*The ball goes in the air.

"Crunch at your core over the ball, and make sure your foot is straight up and down when you strike the ball."

*The ball spins off to the side.

"Make sure your toe is straight down and not turned inward."

*The ball curls across the body.

"Make sure the kicking knee is pushed inward slightly so you strike the ball with the front of the instep—not the inside of the foot."

*The ball digs into the ground before bouncing up into the air—or the player hits the ground with the toe.

"You are hitting the ball too high up on your instep. Make sure you lift your foot, and crunch at the core so you can strike the ball lower on your foot. Also, the lower you strike the ball on the foot, the more force you can generate from the swing."

b) "Dribble forward and shoot on goal. Focus on making the ball hit the goal in the air without spin."

Note: Players should shoot on a target, preferably on a wall or kickback so the ball comes right back to the player, reducing the time retrieving the ball. A few parents standing in the goal can also do the trick to ensure that players can get off as many shots as possible in the time allotted. The object is not to score, but to strike the ball hard at goal. Aiming for corners will come after players learn how to hit a ball with power.

Troubleshooting

*The ball goes across the body and wide of the target.

"You need to take a preparatory touch before the shot so the ball is slightly to the side of the body when you strike the ball. When the ball is too straight in front of you, then the kicking leg is jammed and can't swing properly through the ball with power" (Fig. 5.94i).

Fig. 5.94i

*The ball slices wide.

"The ball is too wide and far away from your kicking foot—don't take the preparatory touch so wide."

"Make sure you keep your toe straight down and not pointed inward toward your body, i.e., pigeon-toed."

COACHING ELEMENT #7 ATTACKING PASSING

Manchester City player David Silva passes forward to create a shot on goal.

Phase of Play	Attacking
Coaching Element	#7 Attacking Passing
Development Stage	I Skills and Tactics
Drill	"Attacking Passing Line Drills"

Learning Objective

Players will learn how to perform wall passes and through balls.

Drill Description

Players line up opposite each other, perform various passing combinations, and follow their passes to the other side.

Player Principles

7.1 The player creating the wall pass "attacks and makes the defender commit" before making the initial pass.

A wall pass is created by one player passing to a teammate who plays a one-touch back to the passer, who has run around and into the space behind a defender. As with 1v1 attacking dribbling, the players initiating the wall pass engage the defenders by dribbling at them and making them commit before passing to the supporting player. If a player passes too early, then the defender will have an easier time turning and dropping back to cover the space where the ball will be played.

7.2 The cues to make a through ball are 1) "space in front of the attacker to look up," 2) "space behind the defense to play the ball," and 3) "a player in position to make the run behind the defense."

Players must recognize important cues to make a through ball so they can react quickly and take advantage of the situation. The through balls are made into spaces behind the defense where players can score or cross the ball in front of the goal.

Skills Introduced

Passing

- Wall passes
- Combination passes
- Through balls

Tactics

- Timed runs behind the defense
- Overlapping runs

Drill Progression

1. Players perform combination passes on each side: short-short-long (Fig. 5.95a).

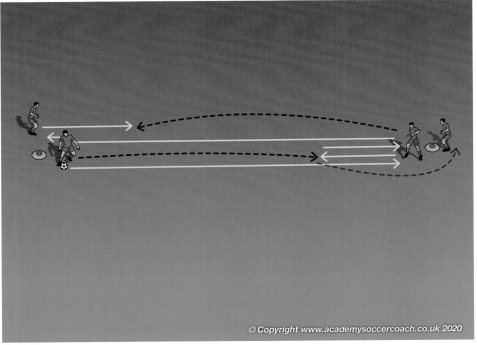

Fig. 5.95a

2. Players perform a wall pass on each side (Fig. 5.95*b*). Initially, players from only one side should do the wall pass.

3. Players perform a combination pass, followed by a wall pass, before passing to the other side and completing the same passing sequence (Fig. 5.95*c*).

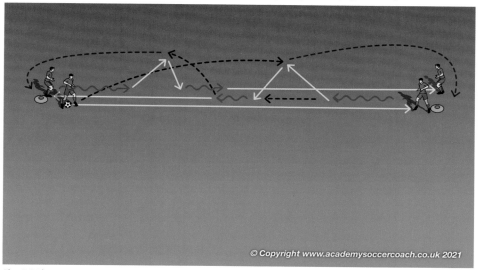

Fig. 5.95b

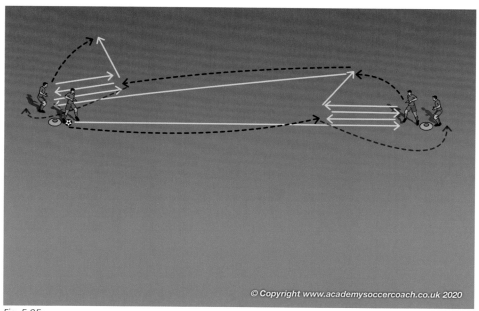

Fig. 5.95c

4. Players perform a combination pass and two wall passes before passing to the other side to complete the same sequence (Fig. 5.95d).

5. Three players perform a wall pass with an overlapping run (Fig. 5.95e).

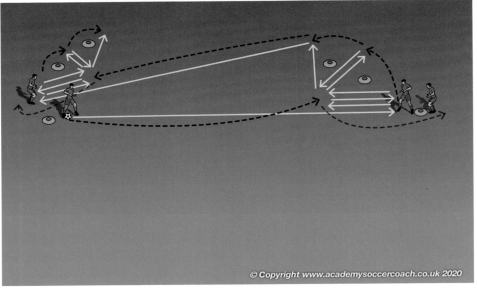

Fig. 5.95d

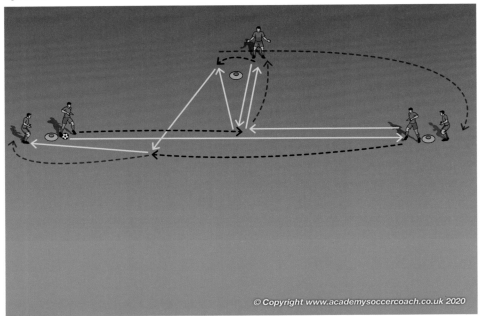

Fig. 5.95e

6.   Players perform a through ball from each direction (Fig. 5.95f).

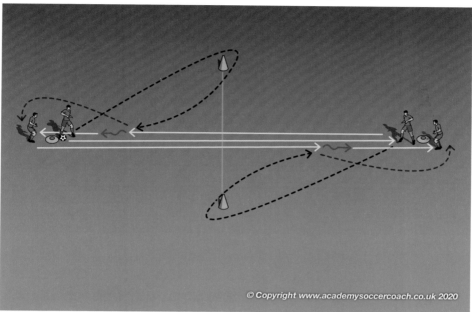

Fig. 5.95f

Coaching Interventions

Problem #1

The wall passes are not performed well.

Possible Cause #1: The players performing the wall pass are using the wrong passing techniques.

Practice Intervention: *Freeze—Demonstrate the proper technique for making a wall pass. Explain that the players can pass the ball with the outside or inside of the foot. The support person, however, will have more success if directly facing the ball and planted while using the inside of the foot to make the wall pass. Players should rehearse the passing technique. *Direct—Within the drill, coach the support player to use the correct technique and "plant" (i.e., stop moving) before passing.

Possible Cause #2: The players doing the wall pass are too far apart or too close to each other.

Practice Intervention *Freeze—Show the players the optimal distance when making a wall pass, say, two to three yards apart. If the support person is too close or too far from the passer, then the one-touch pass can become too challenging to complete.

Possible Cause #3: The passes are too hard or soft.

Practice Intervention: *Freeze—Demonstrate the correct speed of a pass that can be played back one-touch. Explain that harder is not always better when performing wall passes and other combination plays that require one-touch passing. The passes should be firm and crisp, but not overpowering. *Direct—While the players perform the drill, coach them to "increase or decrease the weight of their passes" so they can be handled better by their teammates.

Problem #2
The through balls are not connecting.

Possible Cause #1: The player making the through ball plays the ball too hard or soft, or inaccurately.

Practice Intervention: *Freeze—Demonstrate the proper technique to make a through ball which is accurate and properly weighted so the runner can meet the ball in full stride. The through ball pass is done with a long, smooth leg swing that provides a high level of precision. Players should rehearse the properly weighted pass.

Possible Cause #2: The players making the run are leaving too late or too early or running into the passing lane.

Practice Intervention: *Freeze—Players need to be shown how to run at the right time and angle. The line made between the cones represents the offside line and the runner should not go past the line prior to the pass (Fig. 5.95f). The runner also has to make sure not to cross the center area where the ball will be played, which could result in the ball hitting the runner's heels. The runner should aim to meet the ball at an angle at full speed. *Direct—While the drill is in progress, coach the players to make the run at the right time and angle—"wait, wait, now go."

Possible Cause #3: The player does not communicate about making the run into open space.

Practice Intervention: *Freeze—The runner needs to be shown when and how to communicate. The cue to start the run is for the passer to have the ball under control, with head up. The runner can shout, "Through," or signal with a hand when ready for the pass.

Competitive Game

Wall Pass War—Advanced Drill

Two teams compete against one another in a designated area to see who can get the most points. Use one or two soccer balls at a time, depending on the number of players. Teams score by making five consecutive one-touch passes or completing a wall pass around a player from the other team. Otherwise, there are no touch limitations (Fig. 5.96).

Fig. 5.96

Other Exercises

Open Field Attacking Passing—Easy Drill

All players are in an open area—half of the players have a ball. The players with a ball dribble around and look to play wall passes (A), combination passes (B), combination passing with wall passes (C), and through balls (D) with the players without the ball. Each group with the ball performs one of these passing techniques for one to two minutes before switching with players without a ball. After both groups have done one passing technique, then they each do the next technique for one to two minutes (Fig. 5.97).

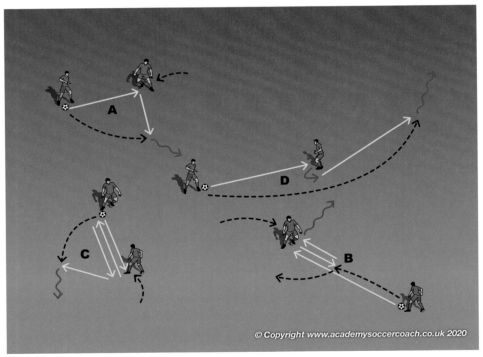

Fig. 5.97

Attacking Passing Around a Square—Moderate Difficultly

Players start on the cones of a square. The ball starts with two players. Advanced groups can use two balls with a minimum of six players starting diagonally from each other. Players pass around the square and perform attacking passing patterns.

Combination Passing

Players perform a combination pass at each cone (Fig. 5.98a).

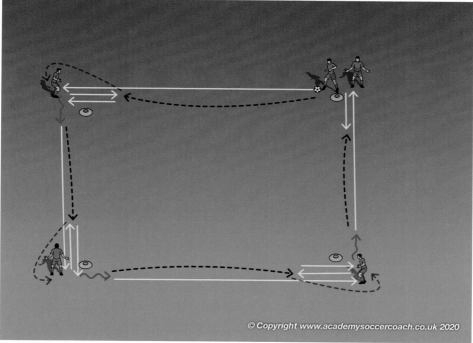

Fig. 5.98a

Wall Passes

Players perform a wall pass at each cone (Fig. 5.98*b*)

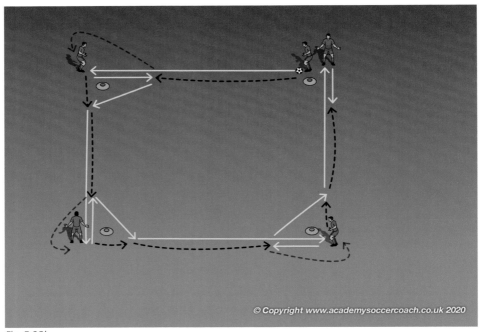

Fig. 5.98b

Off-the-Ball ("Third-Person") Runs

This drill focuses on players making runs to support a pass while not directly involved in the play (Fig. 5.98c).

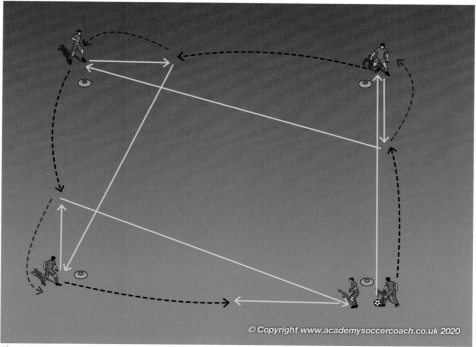

Fig. 5.98c

2v2 Attacking Passing—Advanced Drill

This drill focuses on the exploitation of space. Two players play against two others, with a target player on each end of a rectangular playing area. Each pair of players performs various attacking passing patterns before passing the ball across the field to the target player. The target player will then pass to the two players who had just been defenders. The defending players provide passive defense for the attackers. Passing options are derived from the type of pressure from the defenders.

The ball starts with a target player and the four field players at the side-center cones. The receiver is the player who initially gets the ball from the target player to start the drill. Prior to each passing pattern, you will explain to the players how you want them to defend.

Passing pattern (Fig. 5.99a): Wall pass

*Defense: Tight (on receiver)—Loose (on supporting player)

The first pass is made to the receiver who is under tight pressure from the defender. The pressure leaves space for the receiver to run in behind the defender after performing the wall pass.

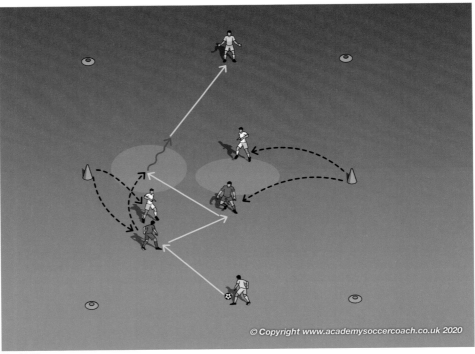

Fig. 5.99a

Passing pattern (Fig. 5.99*b*): Through Ball

*Defense: Loose (on receiver)—Tight (on supporting player)

Under low pressure, the receiver can look forward. The receiver fakes a short pass, drawing in the support person's defender even more, before playing a through ball into the space behind the defender.

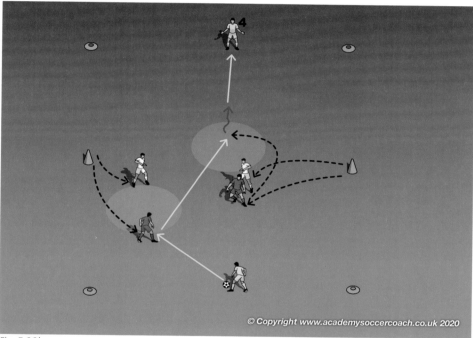

Fig. 5.99b

Passing pattern (Fig. 5.99c):

* Defense: Loose (on receiver)—Loose (on the supporting player)

Players play a combination pass to draw the defenders toward the ball, and then play a through ball into the space created behind the defense.

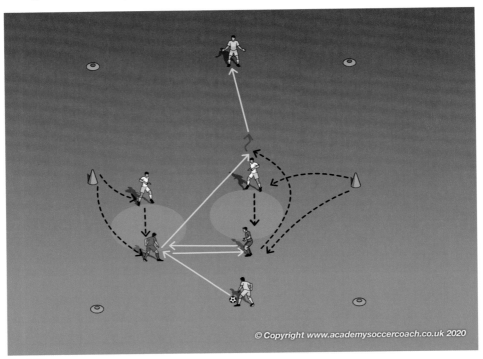

Fig. 5.99c

Passing Pattern (Fig. 5.99*d*):

* Defense: Tight (on receiver)—Tight (on the supporting player)

Players pass to the back foot and retreat to create enough space to look up and to pass a through ball behind the defenders.

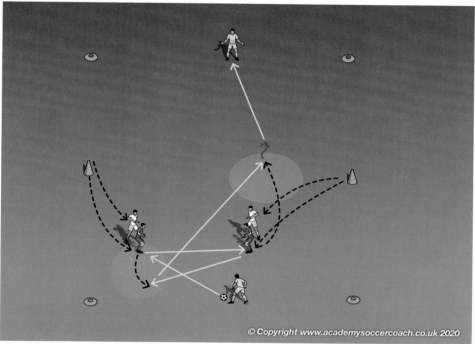

Fig. 5.99d

Attacking Passing Drills to Goal—Moderate Difficulty

Wall passes (A), through balls (B), and combination passing (C) are performed to set up a shot on goal (Fig. 5.100).

Fig. 5.100

Phase of Play	Attacking
Coaching Element	#7 Attacking Passing
Development Stage	II Competitive Game
Drill	5v5+4 Wall Pass and Through Ball End Zone Game"

Learning Objective

Players will learn how to use wall passes and through balls to get behind the defense.

Drill Description

5v5+4

Two teams of five play each other in a 20-yard by 30-yard area. One player from each team remains in the end zone. There are two bumpers on each side of the field who play with the team in possession. Teams score in several ways: 1) passing to a player running into the end zone, 2) making four consecutive one-touch passes, or 3) performing a wall pass. The player in each end zone can defend against the opposing team, but the opposing team cannot steal the ball from the end zone player, who is limited to three touches or two seconds. There are no touch limitations for field players. Bumpers are limited to one touch (Fig. 5.101).

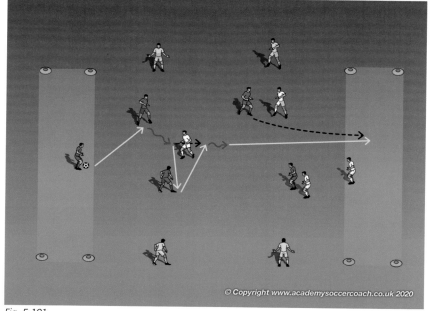

Fig. 5.101

Player Principles

7.3 "Provide support to the dribbler" to create wall pass opportunities.

Players off the ball need to provide the right angle of support to create a wall pass opportunity. The supportive players need to be close enough to receive a pass, but not so close as to get in the way if the attacker on the ball decides to dribble 1v1 against the defender rather than do a wall pass.

7.4 "Quickly get players running behind the defense" when the through pass is possible.

Players need to go forward when the cues for a through ball are present, i.e., the player on the ball has space to look forward and there is space behind the defense into which they can play.

Drill Variations

- Player in the end zone may not defend.
- Players can also (or only) score by dribbling into the end zone.
- There is a three-touch limit for field players.
- Reduce the number of bumpers on the edge of the field.
- Change the depth of the end zone to make it harder or easier to score.
- Keep one player on each team in the attacking half so this player cannot drop back and defend.

Coaching Interventions

Problem #1
The players are unable to create wall passes.

Possible Cause #1: The player on the ball does not engage the defender enough before doing the wall pass.

Practice Intervention: *Demonstrate—Between games, show that the best time to initiate the wall pass is when the defender steps forward to win the ball. *Direct—Coach the players during the game to engage the defender before attempting the wall pass.

Possible Cause #2: Players are not moving into supportive positions to help create opportunities for wall passes.

Practice Intervention: *Direct—During the game, coach the players about when and how to support the player on the ball at the right distance and angle.

Possible Cause #3: Players are not using consecutive one-touch passes to draw defenders out of position.

Practice Intervention: *Direct—Tell players during the game that making short passes will draw the defenders toward the ball, creating space behind the defenders to exploit. *Drill Change—Increase the number of points for consecutive passes.

Problem #2

The attacking teams are not able to score on through balls.

Possible Cause: The players on and off the ball do not recognize the opportunity to make a through ball.

Practice Intervention: *Explain—Between games, remind players of the cues for a through ball—space in front of the passer and behind the defense. *Direct – Point out to players in the game when a through ball is possible.

Problem #3

The attacking team is not utilizing both wall passes and through balls.

Possible Cause: The players are comfortable performing one pass more than the other.

Practice Intervention: *Freeze—Stop the game and show the players opportunities for through balls or wall passes. It is not uncommon for players to use either wall passes or through balls, but not both in a game. Wall passing and through balls are similar in that both free a player behind a defender to attack the goal. However, the set-up to produce each type of pass is very different. In a wall pass, the player on the ball must dribble at a defender to take away the space between them, whereas a through ball can only occur when the player on the ball has ample space to look up and make a pass forward. It takes practice for players to feel comfortable using both passing approaches equally.

*Explain – Discuss with players at restarts what passing style they need to look to do more of in the drill. *Direct – Coach players during the game to encourage wall pass or through ball opportunities. *Drill Change – Make the field wider so it is easier for players to have time on the ball to look forward. Add extra points for the passing approach that the teams are not doing as frequently.

Other Exercises

Rondo With Wall Pass—Advanced Drill

Five players play Rondo against two or three defenders and score by either making seven passes or making a wall pass around a defender. Defenders score by dribbling out of the area or making two or three passes to each other (Fig. 5.102).

Fig. 5.102

Possession With Wall Pass Game—Advanced Drill

Play 8v4 in an area 20 yards by 30 yards. Two attackers stay in the center with six players around the edge. Attackers score by making four one-touch passes or completing a wall pass. Defenders score by winning the ball and scoring a goal on either side of the field or by making three consecutive passes (Fig. 5.103).

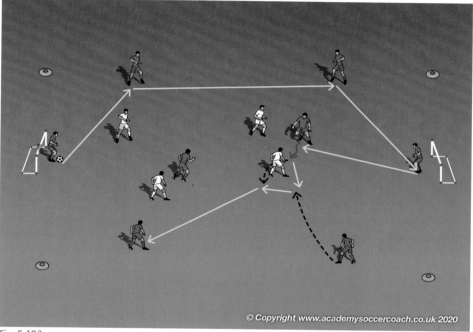

Fig. 5.103

2v2+2 Attacking Passing Game—Moderate Difficulty

Score by passing to a player running into the end zone, completing a wall pass, or making three consecutive one-touch passes. Bumpers play one- or two-touch (Fig. 5.104).

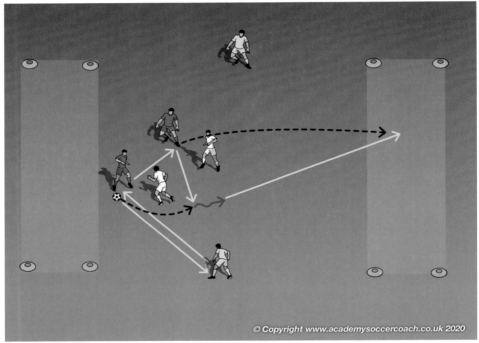

Fig. 5.104

3v3+2 to Goal—Moderate Difficulty

Teams earn points by scoring on the goal (below the waist), making four consecutive one-touch passes, or completing a wall pass. Bumpers play one- or two-touch. One of the three players is a goalkeeper when defending, but moves out some distance into the field to help support the attack (Fig. 5.105).

© Copyright www.academysoccercoach.co.uk 2020

Fig. 5.105

Drill Variation: Take away one or both bumpers.

2v2 to Targets—Advanced Drill

Two teams of two play each other with the objective of passing the ball to the far-side target player (Fig. 5.106). Players can only pass the ball to the target player when they are in the same half as the target player. No long passes are allowed from inside a player's own half. Players can also score by making four one-touch passes. This game uses the same set-up as the drills shown in Fig. 5.99, *a*, *b*, *c*, and *d*.

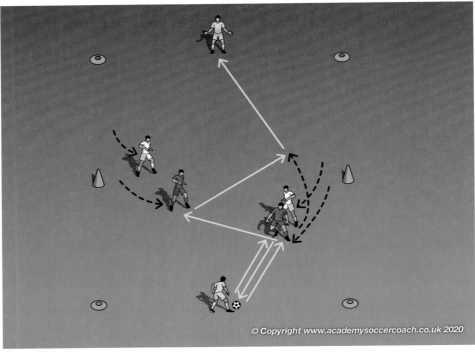

Fig. 5.106

Phase of Play	Attacking
Coaching Element	#7 Attacking Passing
Development Stage	III Positional Game
Drill	"6v5 Attacking Passing Game to End Zone"

Learning Objective

Players will learn how to use wall passes and through balls in a positional game to exploit the space behind defenders.

Drill Description

The attacking team plays in a 3-3 formation against a defense in a 3-2 formation. The attacking team scores by passing the ball into the end zone, completing a wall pass, or completing four one-touch passes. Defenders score by passing through the small goals (Fig. 5.107).

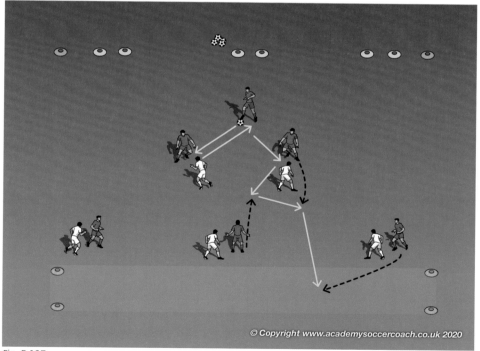

Fig. 5.107

Player Principle
7.5 "Create and exploit overloads."

An overload occurs when the attacking team has more players in an area than the defending team. To create overloads and surprise, players need to move away from their original positions, overlapping or quickly shifting players toward the ball. For example, a 2v1 can be created when a player overlaps another player with the ball or steps toward the ball to set up a wall pass.

Drill Variations

- Have a three-touch limit for attackers.
- Add an extra defender along the back line to play in a 4-2 formation.
- Add two bumpers behind the attackers to help them keep possession.
- Allow the bumpers to join the attack for five seconds, and then they must return to their original positions behind the midfielders. The bumpers start on the sides of the field behind the attackers so they can run forward and overlap the wing forwards. Bumpers are not allowed to defend the small goals.

Coaching Interventions

Problem
The teams do not create opportunities to do wall passes or through balls.

Possible Cause: The attacking players won't leave their positions.

Practice Intervention: *Freeze—Stop the game and show the players where they should move from their positions to create wall passes and through balls. For example, wing forwards can make angled runs toward the center of the field and midfielders can overlap the forwards to receive through balls behind the defense. The center forward can drop into the midfield to offer support to make a wall pass. *Direct—Players often need encouragement to leave their positions, especially if they have been taught by previous coaches never to leave their assigned spots on the field. Within the game, coach the players about where they can make a run to create an attack.

Other Exercises

8v8 Positional Attacking Game to a Standard Goal—Advanced Drill

The attacking team plays in a 2-3-3 versus a defending team in a 4-3+GK in half a field. The attacking team scores on the goal or makes a wall pass or through ball for a point, while the defending team scores on the small goals (Fig. 5.108).

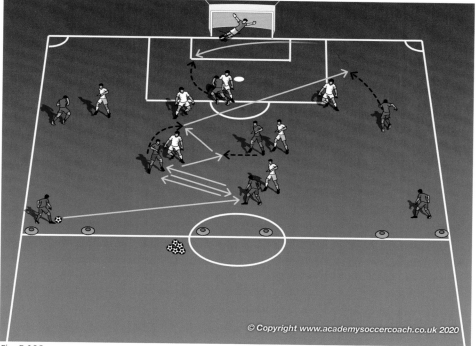

Fig. 5.108

Phase of Play	Attacking
Coaching Element	#7 Attacking Passing
Development Stage	IV Standard Game
Drill	"11v11"

Learning Objective

Using wall passes and through balls, players will improve their ability to create goal-scoring chances in a standard game.

Drill Description

4-3-3 v 4-3-3

While playing in a standard formation, the teams will create attacking opportunities with wall passes, combination passes, and through balls. To provide different challenges to the attacking team, the defense should alternate between pressing up higher toward the halfway line and dropping back in front of the goal.

Player Principle

7.6 Players should look to exploit "third-person runs" to create attacking opportunities.

As the team passes the ball quickly around in the attacking half, the defense is drawn toward the ball, leaving attackers free to make runs behind the defense to receive a pass. The attacker who is left free to make runs off the ball is known as the "third person."

Coaching Interventions

Problem
The team does not create goal-scoring opportunities.

Possible Cause: Players off the ball are stationary and do not offer support to the player with the ball or make runs behind the defense.

Practice Intervention: *Direct—Coach the team to perform combination passes to attract defenders to the ball in order to create space for attackers to run behind the defense. Direct players to make runs away from the ball and remind players on the ball to get their heads up to scan the field for forward passes and the possibility to create a wall pass. *Freeze—Stop the game and demonstrate how players can transition from probing to attacking through off-the-ball runs and combination passing. Players should rehearse making a pass to a "third person" after a series of short passes that draws in the defense.

Alternate Formations

9v9 Formation
3-2-3 v 3-2-3

Three forwards on each team give the teams opportunities to perform wall passes and through balls.

7v7 Formation
2-3-1 v 2-3-1

The outside midfielders will push forward to create opportunities for wall passes and through balls in the attacking half.

5v5 Formation
2-2 v 2-2

The two forwards will combine to create attacking passing opportunities.

SKILLS FOR ATTACKING PASSING

CHIPPING

The chip is an ideal way to pass a ball in the air to a player running down the field. The chip creates a strong backspin on the ball which will slow the ball down after it lands.

1 Soccer Position

"Stand with your feet facing forward, knees softly bent, feet just wider than shoulder width, engaged at the core" (Figs. 3.1, *a* and *b*).

2 Grounded Skill Position

"Turn the kicking toe outward and place the kicking leg out to the side with both knees bent deeply so the kicking foot can angle forward to create a wedge. The kicking foot is in line with the heel of the planting foot. The inner edge of the kicking foot and heel should be touching the ground. The kicking foot should touch the ball at the end of the foot (top of the toe knuckles)" (Fig. 5.109).

Fig. 5.109

3 Skill

a) "Run up to the stationary ball at a 45-degree angle and chip the ball to your partner. The ball should shoot upward with lots of backspin."

b) "Chip the ball that is moving."

c) "Dribble in one direction, make a quick turn and chip the moving ball toward your partner."

Troubleshooting

*The ball does not go into the air.

"Keep the inside of the heel and big toe flat to the ground with the toe pointed outward, so the foot can angle forward. Strike the ball with the lowest part of the foot. You cannot get under the ball kicking with the thicker instep. Make sure the ball is not too far in front of you when you strike it."

*The ball curls across the body and does not fly straight to the target.

"Keep your toe down when you strike the ball. The ball will curl away if the toe lifts up when kicking the ball."

Outside-of-the-Foot Chip

The outside-of-the-foot chip is a dynamic and elegant way to connect to a player running behind the defense with a pass that curls into the player's path. The run up to the outside-of-the-foot chip is straight on, despite the instinct to run up to the ball from the side, as in the chip. Again, the foot strikes very low on the ball. Generally, only players 12 years old and older should practice this skill, as it takes a good deal of leg muscle that younger, undeveloped players do not generally have to chip the ball at this awkward leg and foot angle.

1 Soccer Position

"Stand with your feet facing forward, knees softly bent, feet just wider than shoulder width, engaged at the core" (Figs. 3.1, *a* and *b*).

2 Open Skill Position

"Standing directly behind the ball, angle the kicking foot down and inward with knees bent. The end of the angled, kicking foot (top of the smallest toe knuckles) should touch the ball at the ball's lowest point. The kicking foot is at a low angle to the ground with the heel of the kicking foot only a couple of inches off the ground. The body is slightly leaning back" (Fig. 5.110).

Fig. 5.110

294

3 Skill

a) "Standing still behind the ball, snap down with your leg, and chip the ball 15 yards to your partner with the outside of the foot." (Players should try to chip the ball to head height.)

b) "Run straight at the stationary ball. With your foot turned inward and angled down, strike low on the ball, chipping the ball with an outside curve toward your partner."

c) "Do the outside-of-the-foot chip with a moving ball."

d) "Dribble in one direction, perform a quick turn, and do an outside-of-the-foot chip with a moving ball."

Troubleshooting

*The ball does not go into the air.

"Run straight at the ball and angle the foot, not the body. Snap the lower leg so the top of the smallest toe knuckles of the kicking foot strikes the lowest part of the ball. Don't lift from the hip."

COACHING ELEMENT #8 CROSSING

picture alliance / dpa | Rolf Vennenbernd

Celia Okoyino Da Mbabi of Germany heads a cross on goal.

Phase of Play	Attacking
Coaching Element	#8 Crossing
Development Stage	I Skills and Tactics
Drill	"Crossing and Finishing"

Learning Objective

Players will learn the techniques needed to cross a ball into the penalty box and finish on goal.

Drill Description

A center player passes to a wing player who dribbles down the sideline before crossing the ball into the center of the goal, where players are making runs to the near and far posts (Fig. 5.111a).

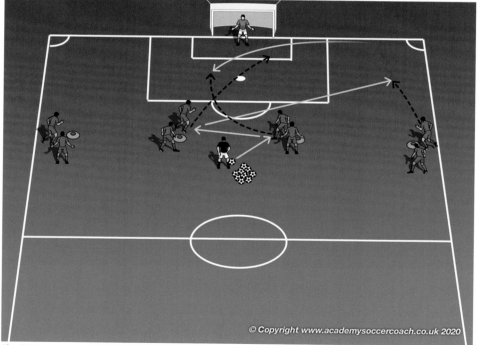

Fig. 5.111a

Player Principles

8.1 The crosser should "dribble to the end line before making the cross" with the "final dribble angled toward the goal."

When crossing from the end line, the crosser keeps everybody onside and provides an angled pass back to the runners who can more easily redirect the ball toward goal. The last touch before the cross should be toward the goal, to make it easier to cross the ball away from the goalkeeper and back toward the players running into the penalty box.

8.2 Crossers should "pick out the runners."

Players need to look up prior to making a cross to pick out an open runner.

8.3 Attackers need to "leave late and arrive on time" when making runs into the box.

Attackers need to be patient so that they arrive in the penalty box at the same time that the cross arrives. Arriving too early will allow the defenders to catch up and block the cross. Attackers should wait until the crosser looks up before sprinting to the area in the box where they want to meet the ball.

8.4 Attackers should fill important parts of the goal area by "running to the near and far posts and the penalty spot."

Attackers need to be in areas where the ball is likely to be crossed, but they should not all run to the same part of the goal area. The first runner, the player in front, dictates where the others will go. If the first runner runs to the near post, then the second and third runners need to fill in the far post and penalty mark areas. The player running to the near post generally gets closer to the goal than the player running to the far post, who hangs back more. The far post run is important for long, lofted crosses, whereas a near-post run is important for low, hard crosses. Runners to the penalty spot should look for the cut-back pass.

Attackers should adjust their runs if the crosser decides to dribble down the end line toward the goal, creating different angles. One solution is for the player on the near post to pull back away from the goal to create space to receive the pass and the player on the far post to run in close to the goal to look for space for a pass behind the defense (Fig 5.111*b*).

Fig. 5.111b

8.5 Attackers need to volley hard crosses with a "big foot, not a big swing."

Attackers should not over-hit a hard cross but seek to make firm contact with the ball with the inside of the foot meeting the ball with a short swing. This technical principle is true for hard crosses in the air and on the ground.

8.6 Players should keep the "heel over the ball" when performing a side volley.

Players need to get the heel over the midpoint of the ball to help ensure the shot stays low and does not go over the goal. This is true for volleying the ball out of the air and striking a rolling ball with the instep using the squib pass technique.

8.7 If possible, head the ball "down toward the goal line."

Heading the ball down will keep it away from the goalkeeper's hands. Of course, there are exceptions, such as when the best option is to redirect the ball straight into the goal or loft the ball over the goalkeeper.

8.8 Crosses that cannot be shot on goal should be "redirected back to the center of the goal" for another player to finish.

Players should play the ball back to the center of the goal with the feet or head if they are not in a position to score directly. Players off the ball should be prepared for this back pass.

Skills Introduced
Passing

- Crossing

Finishing

- Side volley
- Inside-of-the-foot volley
- One-touch shots from crosses played on the ground
- Heading

Drill Progression

1. Volleying technical training: Prior to doing crossing drills, players should practice inside-of-the-foot volleying and heading techniques using drills similar to those for trapping (See Fig. 5.35, *a* and *b*). To practice side volleys, have players toss the ball up in the air, let the ball bounce, and, when the ball is waist high, strike the ball with the top of the instep toward a partner, wall or goal.

2. Finishing training: Players practice shooting techniques on goal with the coach first throwing or passing the ball from close range to players running into the penalty box. The distance of the cross should increase as the players show improvement.

3. Players dribble down the sideline and cross the ball on the ground to players running into the penalty box.

4. Players dribble down the sideline and cross the ball in the air to players making runs in the penalty box.

5. Players dribble down the sideline and cut down the end line toward the goal, forcing the runners to change their positions.

6.   A defender who marks one attacker is added, forcing the crosser to pick out an open runner.

7.   The crosser plays the ball long to the far post, so the runner has to head or volley the ball back into the middle of the goal area for another attacker to finish.

Drill Variations

- Change the number of players who run into the box.
- Change the spot where the runs start.
- The crosser has to do dribbling moves through cones before making the cross.

Coaching Interventions

Problem #1

The crosses are not good enough to create goal-scoring opportunities.

Possible Cause: The crosser lacks the skills to play the cross into the goal area.

Practice Intervention: *Freeze—Demonstrate the right technique to aim a lofted or grounded ball away from the goalkeeper. *Direct—While the crossers are dribbling down the field, remind them to take the last touch toward the goal so it will be easier to cross the ball away from the goalkeeper. *Drill Change—1) Add cones to the field where the player should begin to angle the dribble toward the goal; 2) move the crosser in closer to the goal to make the cross easier; 3) reduce the distance the attacker has to dribble before making the cross; 4) keep crosses on the ground; 5) have the crosser practice crossing with a still ball; and 6) the youngest players can dribble down to the end line, pick the ball up with their hands, and kick the ball out of their hands into the penalty box. This last option is not very realistic for the crosser, but the attackers get a chance to work on volleys, which they normally would not do because players at their age typically cannot chip the ball very high or far.

Problem #2

The attackers are not able to finish the crosses on goal.

Possible Cause #1: The runners in the penalty box use the wrong technique to score on goal.

Practice Intervention: *Freeze—Demonstrate the correct technique for scoring on goal when the ball is played in various ways: lofted (instep volley/header), driven (inside of foot redirected), or passed on the ground (angled instep, i.e., squib). *Direct—Coach the players to use the correct technique based on the type of cross.

Possible Cause #2: The attackers make the wrong type of run into the penalty box.

Practice Intervention: *Drill Change—Place poly spot markers in the penalty box where you want players to run and meet the cross.

Competitive Game

Crossing Game—Advanced Drill

The attacking team keeps track of how many goals it can score during the initial drill (Fig. 5.111*a*) against a defender and a goalkeeper. The attackers get a point for scoring directly off a cross, and the defenders receive a point for clearing the ball out of the penalty box in the air. Adjust the number of defenders and attackers to ensure competitiveness.

Phase of Play	Attacking
Coaching Element	#8 Crossing
Development Stage	II Competitive Game
Drill	"Crossing Game With Channels"

Learning Objective

Players will learn how to use crosses to create goal-scoring opportunities in a competitive game.

Drill Description

5v5+2

Teams play a small-sided game to two standard goals with neutral side channels where bumpers are free to cross the ball, without pressure, into the penalty box. Teams score three points for a crossing goal and one point for a goal scored through central play (Fig. 5.112).

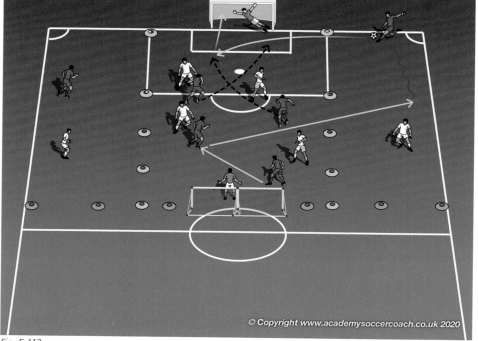

Fig. 5.112

303

Player Principle

8.9 Players need to "elude defenders to get free for crosses."

Players running into the penalty box for a cross should curve their runs and change speeds to get free of the defenders. Straight runs are more predictable and easier to cover.

Drill Variations

- Limit time for bumpers to cross the ball.
- Add extra points if the attacking team can score on a "double volley," where one player heads a cross back across the goal to a teammate who scores on a one-touch volley or header.
- Eliminate bumpers and play 6v6 (including GK), but players can dribble into the neutral areas where they have three seconds to cross the ball without pressure.

Coaching Interventions

Problem

The teams do not create goal-scoring opportunities through crosses.

Possible Cause #1: The players making runs do not get free to receive the crosses.

Practice Intervention: *Demonstrate—Between games, show 1) how to elude defenders in the penalty box by making timed, curved and jagged runs that play off the back shoulder of the defender, making attacking players more difficult to mark, 2) how to recycle or alter runs if the dribbler is delayed or is able to dribble down the end line, and 3) how the crosser should look up and pick out the open runner. *Direct—During the game, coach the players when and how to make deceptive runs. *Drill Change—Reduce the number of defenders who can be in the penalty box to defend the goal, making it easier for the attackers to get open to score.

Possible Cause #2: The crosses are too flat, high, hard, and inaccurate to create goal-scoring chances for attackers.

Practice Intervention: *Explanation—Between games, review the appropriate techniques for crossing the ball accurately in various situations—lofted cross to the far post; hard, low cross to the near post; cut-back pass to the center of the goal area; and firm pass along the ground behind the defense. Remind players about the importance of angling the last dribble toward the goal in order to cross the ball away from the goalkeeper.

Possible Cause #3: The teams do not look wide to the bumpers to make the cross.

Practice Intervention: *Direct—Coach the players during the game when they should pass the ball wide. Explain why playing the ball wide is advantageous—there are fewer players out wide and more space than in the middle of the field for attackers to advance the ball up the field. Tell bumpers to communicate more when they are open to receive a pass. *Game Change—Increase the number of points for goals scored off crosses in order to incentivize playing the ball wide.

Possible Cause #4: The shots on goal are inaccurate.

Practice Intervention: *Direct—As the ball is coming across, coach the players to use the right technique: "Big foot, not big swing," "Redirect the ball," "Heel over the ball," and "Watch the ball strike your foot."

Phase of Play	Attacking
Coaching Element	#8 Crossing
Development Stage	III Positional Game
Drill	"Positional Crossing Game With Channels"

Learning Objective

Players will learn how to create goal-scoring opportunities from wide areas while playing in standard positions.

Drill Description

8v7 (including the GK)

The attacking team plays in a 2-3-3 formation while the defending team plays in a 4-2 formation. Channels are outlined on the sides of the field. The attacking team can score directly through the center of the field or from a cross for added points. An attacking player can have three seconds in the side channel before a defender can pressure the ball. The defending team scores on small goals or any clearance from a cross that is in the air when it leaves the penalty box (Fig. 5.113).

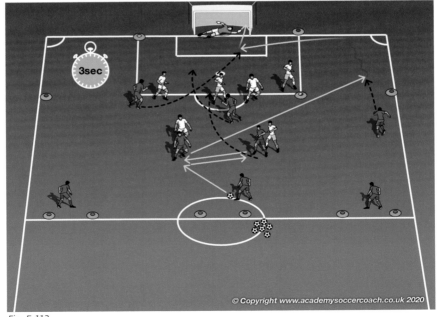

Fig. 5.113

Player Principle

8.10 The attacking team can "create overloads in the channels with overlapping runs."

The attacking team can create chances to cross by using overlaps to create 2v1s in the channels. Midfielders and other forwards can make these overlapping runs, but these runs are often best made by outside fullbacks.

Drill Progression

1. Initially, once they enter the channel the attacking players have three seconds to cross the ball before the defenders can enter the channel to defend the cross.
2. The defending team can enter the channel with only one player at a time, while the attacking team can have multiple players enter the channel.
3. The channels are removed, allowing defending players to move about freely to defend crosses.

Drill Variations

- Widen or shrink the channels to make it easier or harder for the attackers to cross the ball.
- Add an extra defensive center midfielder to make central attacks harder and force the attackers to attempt more crosses from wide areas.

Coaching Interventions

Problem
The attacking team does not make crosses into the penalty box.

Possible Cause: The attacking team is not creating situations where wide players can provide crosses.

Practice Intervention: *Freeze—Stop the game and show the team how to use through balls, switching the field of play, wall passes, overlaps, and third person runs to create crossing opportunities. *Game Changes—1) Reduce the number of defenders and 2) make the channels wider.

Phase of Play	Attacking
Coaching Element	#8 Crossing
Development Stage	IV Standard Game
Drill	"11v11"

Learning Objective

Players will improve their ability to create goal-scoring chances from wide areas in a standard game.

Drill Description

4-3-3 v 4-3-3

Both teams play with three forwards to encourage play in wide areas of the field where players can make crosses.

Player Principle

8.11 Teams need to get "numbers in the box" when a crossing opportunity occurs.

The chances of scoring a goal go up significantly when multiple players get into the penalty box for a cross.

Coaching Interventions

Problem

The teams do not create shots on goal from crosses.

Possible Cause: Not enough attacking players make runs into the penalty box when a cross is made.

Practice Intervention: *Freeze—Stop the game and show how probing in the attacking half can prepare the team to have many players available to run into the penalty box at the time of a cross. *Direct—Coach the specific players who tend to hang back when they should make runs into the penalty box. *Drill Change—Make a rule that goals count extra if a team scores on a cross with four or more players in the box.

Alternate formations

9v9 Formation
3-2-3 v 3-2-3

The use of three forwards ensures width in attack.

7v7 Formation
2-1-3 v 2-1-3

As an alternative, you could play a 2-3-1 so the midfielders have to push forward in wide areas.

5v5 Formation
2-2 v 2-2

In this system, one of the fullbacks should push forward into wide areas to support the attack.

Alternatively, you could play a 1-2-1, where the midfielders have to push forward into wide areas.

Skills for Attacking Crossing

Crossing
"Crossing a ball is similar to the chip, but the toe will lift slightly so that the ball can curl away from the goalkeeper with more power."

Side Volley
The side volley is one of the most exciting shots in soccer. The side volley can generate a lot of power and is best for crosses that are softer, since a hard, low cross can simply be redirected toward goal with a firm inside-of-the-foot volley. The trick to the side volley is to get the leg up high to the side, while also keeping the head above the ball as the torso leans away for balance.

1 Soccer Position

"Stand with your feet facing forward, knees softly bent, feet just wider than shoulder width, engaged at the core" (Figs. 3.1, *a* and *b*).

2 Open Skill Position

a) "Lift the kicking leg up to the side with both knees bent, so that the kicking leg is parallel to the ground, with the top of the foot facing forward toward the target with a firm ankle. Lean the torso away from the kicking leg while keeping the back straight and in line with the kicking leg, with the head higher than the height of the kicking foot" (Fig. 5.114).

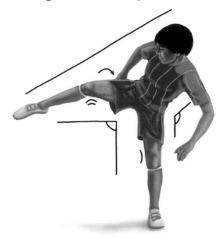

Fig. 5.114

b) "In the side volley position, snap the lower leg as if striking an imaginary ball with the instep."

3 Skill

a) "Throw the ball straight up into the air, let it bounce off the ground and side-volley the ball when it rises to hip height. Make sure to strike the ball at hip level—not near the ground."

b) "The partner throws the ball from the side and the kicker volleys the ball at hip level toward a goal/wall."

c) "The partner chips the ball to the kicker who strikes the ball at a target with the side volley."

Squib Shot

The squib shot is the same technique as the squib pass. See Fig. 5.19, *a* and *b*.

1 Skill

"You should strike a low cross that skims on the ground across the goal with the full instep which 'wraps around the ball.' Make sure the heel stays above the centerline of the ball so that the ball stays low."

Attacking Heading

1 Soccer Position

"Stand with your feet facing forward, knees softly bent, feet just wider than shoulder width, engaged at the core" (Figs. 3.1, *a* and *b*).

2 Open Skill Position

a) "Tuck your chin, keep your eyes open, mouth closed, arms bent to the side, knees bent, legs in a straddle position, and lean back from the waist before snapping forward forcibly" (Fig. 5.115).

b) "Now, jump up and snap forward while in the air."

Fig. 5.115

3 Skill

a) "The partner throws the ball, and the player heads the ball back using the forehead to strike the ball downward toward the partner's feet."

b) "The partner throws the ball higher so the player has to jump up and head the ball back at the partner, making sure the ball goes down. The player heading should hang in the air for a bit before snapping forward at the waist to head the ball."

c) "The player checks to the ball, plants and jumps into the air to perform a header."

d) "Throw the ball from the side so the player has to jump and angle the header toward a target."

COACHING ELEMENT #9 COUNTERATTACKING

Lieke Martens of the Netherlands quickly dribbles forward toward the goal.

Phase of Play	Attacking
Coaching Element	#9 Counterattacking
Development Stage	I Skills and Tactics
Drill	"Counterattacking Passing Pattern"

Learning Objective

Players will learn to play quickly up the field to create a shot on goal.

Drill Description

Groups of players will pass the ball through a variety of patterns, starting from their defensive half and ending with a shot on goal. This drill should be done on a standard soccer field when possible (Fig. 5.116, *a*, *b*, and *c*).

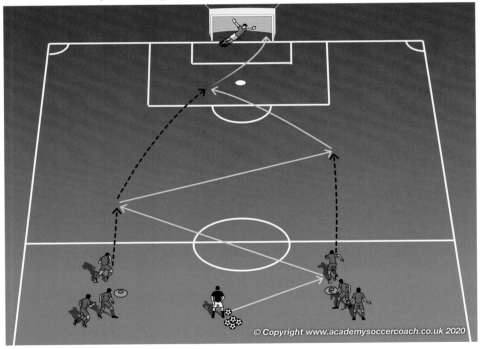

Fig. 5.116a

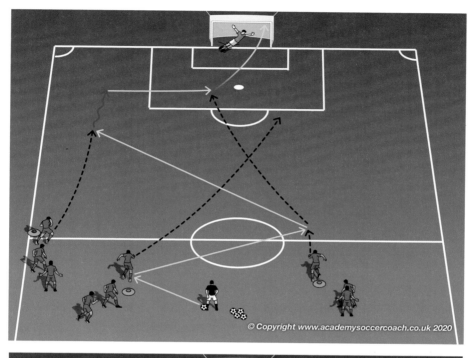

Fig. 5.116, b and c

Player Principles

9.1 Attacking players must "play quickly up the field."

A counterattack only works at high speed, since the attack relies on the attacking team's maintaining numerical advantage against an opponent who does not have the time to get numbers back in defense and reorganized. With energizing, motivational instructions, the coach should actively encourage fast play during this drill.

"I want to see players go as fast as possible once we start the drill. Counterattacking is about surprise, about catching the defense off guard and taking advantage of their disorganization and gaps in coverage. Every second we waste gives the opponent more time to recover. So I need to see 100% effort to move the ball forward from our half into the opponents' half to create a shot on goal as quickly as possible."

9.2 Whenever possible, attacking players should "pass the ball into space" in front of teammates running forward so that the attacking player receiving the ball does not lose momentum.

In a counterattacking play, passes to feet will slow the speed of play because the receiver will have to wait for the ball to arrive before going forward. The counterattack's effectiveness is directly related to the speed at which the team can advance the ball forward.

Skills Introduced

Dribbling

- Fast, straight dribbling in open space

Passing

- Passing into the path of a sprinting player

Shooting

- 1v1 with goalkeepers

Drill Progression

1. Start the drill without defensive pressure.

2. Add defenders who are instructed to create light resistance and block passing lanes.

3. Add a time limit to take a shot on goal.

Drill Variations

-   Change where the ball starts.
-   Change where the attackers start.

Coaching Interventions

Problem

The counterattacks are too slow.

Possible Cause: The players off the ball do not get up the field ahead of the ball quickly enough.

Practice Intervention: *Direct—Coach players to sprint into supporting positions.

Competitive Games

Counterattacking with Defensive Pressure—Moderate Difficulty

Instruct the defenders to stop the attacking team from scoring.

1v1 Chase—Easy Drill

The coach plays a ball into space for an attacker to dribble 1v1 on goal, with the defender starting a couple of yards back. The defender attempts to catch up to the attacker before the attacker can shoot on goal.

The attacker can buy time by dribbling in front of the chaser and cutting off the chaser's direct path to the ball and goal.

The attacker has several options when dribbling 1v1 against the goalkeeper. If the goalkeeper comes far off the goal line, the attacker can attempt to dribble past the goalkeeper. The attacker can also fake a shot in order to get the goalkeeper to dive to the ground and then chip the ball over the goalkeeper into the goal. Lastly, the attacker could pass the ball directly into the goal if the goalkeeper does not come off the line far enough to block the attacker's shooting angle (Fig. 5.117).

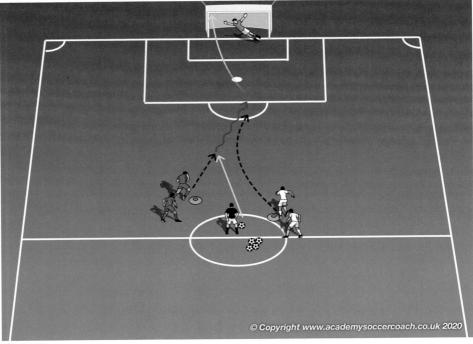

Fig. 5.117

Phase of Play	Attacking
Coaching Element	#9 Counterattacking
Development Stage	II Competitive Game
Drill	"5v5 Counterattack Game to End Zone"

Learning Objective

Players will learn how to quickly counterattack after winning the ball in their defensive half.

Drill Description

5v5

Teams defend in a 3-2 formation, attack in a 2-3 formation, and attempt to score by passing the ball to a player running into the end zone. Goals only count if all five players are in the opponent's attacking half or if the attackers score within a certain time after winning the ball, say, under 10 seconds.

This drill should be done on a standard field with the penalty boxes acting as the end zone and marking the width of the playing field (Fig. 5.118).

Note: The rule requiring all players to be in the attacking half ensures that players have to push forward into it, which leaves space behind them for the other team to counterattack. Without the rule, players might hang back, taking away the space to counterattack. Play with the offside rule.

Fig. 5.118

Player Principles

9.3 Teams need to "quickly transition to counterattacking" when they win the ball.

The team winning the ball must decide immediately if they can counterattack and catch the opponent off guard, or if they should play more conservatively and focus on maintaining possession of the ball.

9.4 As they run forward, the supporting players need to "fill gaps" between defenders to give the player on the ball passing options, to make themselves harder to mark, and to be available for through balls and early crosses.

The counterattacking players off the ball need to fan out and find open areas to run where they can more easily receive passes and cause trouble for the defense. Players need to avoid clumping when they run forward because clumping will make it easier for the defense to cover players and block passing lanes.

9.5 The counterattacking player on the ball should look to "pass early" to supporting players running forward. The "ball runs faster than any player," and passing forward is quicker than players dribbling forward.

In a counterattack, players do not need to wait for pressure to pass the ball, but instead should look for the fastest way forward, which will often involve passing to players ahead of them who are running into open spaces.

Drill Variations

- Add more players to each team.
- Widen or shorten the field to make it easier to score.

Coaching Interventions

Problem
The counterattacks do not result in getting into the end zone.

Possible Cause #1: The players off the ball fail to run into gaps where they can create good passing options.

Practice Intervention: *Explain—Between games, discuss how supporting players need to fill gaps and confuse the defenders with overlapping runs. *Direct—Coach the players within the drill where to run to get away from the defenders.

Possible Cause #2: The players are not fit enough to sustain a counterattack at a full sprint.

Practice Intervention: *Drill Change—1) Shorten the field or 2) create longer breaks between games. Players must sprint 100% when they do the counterattack. Performing a counterattack in a fatigued state will reinforce the wrong behaviors.

Phase of Play	Attacking
Coaching Element	#9 Counterattacking
Development Stage	III Positional Game
Drill	"10v10 Counterattack to a Standard Goal"

Learning Objective

Players will learn how to counterattack for a goal from standard game positions.

Drill Description

10v10 (including GKs)

The teams will attack in a 2-4-3 and defend in a 4-3-2. Teams can only score when they have seven attacking players in the "final third" (within 30 yards of the goal) or score off a counterattack in ten seconds. The drill restarts at the halfway line with one team in a deep defensive position (Fig. 5.119).

Fig. 5.119

Player Principle

9.6 Attacking players should take advantage of the open space and numerical advantage on the counterattack to "create high-percentage shots on goal."

Counterattacking players should not necessarily take the first shot possible, especially from a distance, since they will often be able to create higher-percentage goal-scoring opportunities with players who are able to get behind the defense or trail the attack.

Coaching Interventions

Problem

The counterattacking team fails to score.

Possible Cause: The counterattacking team does not create high-percentage shots on goal.

Practice Intervention: *Freeze—Stop the game and remind players not to always take the first shot on goal, but to first look to see if they can create a higher-percentage shot on goal. Show players where to make passes that create better angles to score on goal. Supporting players should never give up on the play, but rather should keep running into gaps to offer support for the player on the ball. Even when a player breaks free and is 1v1 with the goalkeeper, a supportive player should run along in support of the dribbler to provide another angle to score on goal. *Explain—Discuss player shooting choices during restarts. *Direct—Coach players within the game how they can create a higher-percentage shot on goal. Encourage support players not to give up on the play.

Phase of Play	Attacking
Coaching Element	#9 Counterattacking
Development Stage	IV Standard Game
Drill	"11v11"

Learning Objective

Players will learn how to counterattack in a standard game.

Drill Description

4-3-3 v 4-3-3

The teams are instructed to defend deep in their defensive half in order to create the space to counterattack.

Player Principle

9.7 Teams need to choose whether to "build up or counterattack" when they win the ball in their defensive half.

In a standard game, teams will have to decide when to build up for an attack and when to launch a counterattack. It is also possible to transition to a counterattack after trying to build up from the back if the opponent attempts to press the ball, leaving gaps behind the midfielders where the attacking team could start a quick counterattack.

Coaching Interventions

Problem

The teams do not create counterattacking opportunities.

Possible Cause: The teams are too conservative and mostly choose to slowly build up rather than quickly counterattack when they win the ball.

Practice Intervention: *Freeze—Stop the game and show the scenarios in which counterattacking is the right choice after winning the ball, such as when the opposing team is disorganized and has many players pushed forward. *Direct—Coach the players within the game when to counterattack.

Alternate Formations

9v9 Formation
3-3-2 v 3-3-2

The teams will defend in a 3-3 and counterattack through the two forwards.

7v7 Formation
2-3-1 v 2-3-1

The teams will need to push the outside midfielders forward in the counterattack.

5v5 Formation
1-2-1 v 1-2-1

At least one of the midfielders will need to push forward and join the counterattack.

COACHING ELEMENT #10 BLOCK-ZONAL DEFENDING

picture alliance/dpa | Sebastian Gollnow

US players Julie Ertz, Samantha Mewis, and Becky Sauerbrunn defend the goal.

Phase of Play	Defending
Coaching Element	#10 Block-Zonal Defending
Development Stage	I Skills and Tactics
Drill	"1v1 – 4v4 Shadow Defending"

Learning Objective

Players will learn block-zonal defending principles in 1v1, 2v1, 2v2, 3v3, and 4v4 situations.

Drill Description

The defense will pass to the offense and run up to defend. After engaging the attacking players, the defensive players jockey back in a defensive stance before letting the attackers go past to the other side. Attackers do not try to get around the defender, but dribble and pass the ball among themselves while advancing the ball forward. Defenders focus on their positioning as the ball moves side to side and up and down the field.

Player Principles

10.1 Defending players must "put pressure on the ball."

The first principle of defense is to put pressure on the ball. Without pressure, the attacker is free to pass, shoot, and dribble to set up goals.

The defenders need to run up quickly to the attacker and then slow down with small, active steps. By angling their bodies to force play one way or another, the defenders can make the attackers' dribbling more predictable. The angled stance allows the defender to turn quickly if the attacker attempts to dribble past. An angled stance also makes the defender less likely to have the ball played through the legs. The pressuring defender's distance to the attacker should be a bit more than arm's length away so that the defender is close enough to block a direct shot or pass, but not so close that the attacker can easily dribble past. As the attacker dribbles, the defender should maintain the same arm's-length distance, possibly switching the angle of the defending stance when the attacker changes dribbling directions from side to side.

10.2 Defending players need to "provide cover for the pressure on the ball."

The second defender needs to get into a supporting position to provide cover for the defender pressuring the ball.

If the covering player is too far away from the pressuring defender, then the attacker has time to look up after dribbling around the pressuring defender before confronting the covering defender. This gives the attacker a better chance to make a pass or dribble around the covering defender (Fig. 5.120*a*).

Fig. 5.120a

If the defenders are even with one another in a line, then the attacker can make one dribbling move to beat both defenders (Fig. 5.120*b*).

Fig. 5.120b

10.3 Other defenders must "support the cover on the ball."

The remaining defenders in the block defense line need to fan out and support the pressure and cover on the ball, while also blocking passing lanes across the field. While the covering defender provides close help to the pressuring defender, the supportive players guard important spaces away from the ball. The positions of the supporting defenders depend on the location of the ball. Central attacks are defended in a V shape, formation and attacks along the outside are defended with a curled line. The supporting defenders should not be in a straight line with the covering and pressuring defenders, or one pass easily can cut out all the defenders.

10.4 Defending players must constantly "adjust their positioning as the ball moves."

As the attackers move the ball around, the defense line needs to slide in unison from side to side to keep pressure on the ball and provide support and cover for the pressuring defender. As the ball moves, the roles of the defenders change from pressuring to covering to supporting.

Skills Introduced

Tactics

- Closing down and pressuring attackers
- Block-zonal defending shape and movements
- Tackling
- Shot and pass blocking
- Clearing the ball: defensive heading and inside-of-the-foot volley

Drill Progression

1. Put pressure on the ball.

   One defender defends against one attacker (Fig. 5.121).

Fig. 5.121

2.   Defenders provide cover.

Two defenders go against one attacker. One defender pressures the ball, and the second defender provides cover in case the attacker dribbles around the pressuring defender (Fig. 5.122).

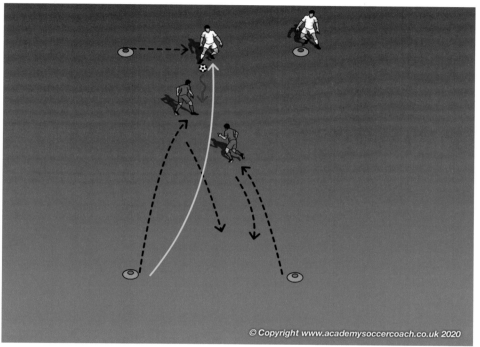

Fig. 5.122

3.   The defenders switch roles.

Two defenders challenge two attackers. The defenders switch from providing pressure to providing cover as the ball is passed between the attackers (Fig. 5.123).

Fig. 5.123

4.   A third defender provides support.

Three defenders face three attackers. The additional defender supports the covering and pressuring defenders (Fig. 5.124, *a* and *b*).

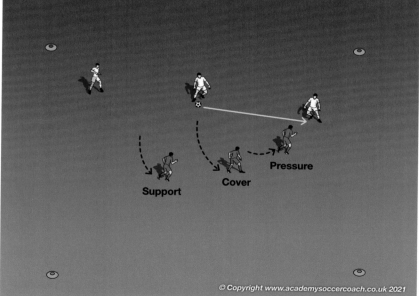

Fig. 5.124, a and b

5. A fourth defender provides additional support.

Four defenders go against four attackers. A typical defensive line in a standard game would include four defenders. The fourth defender adds even more support for the covering and pressuring defenders (Fig. 5.125, *a*, *b*, *c* and *d*).

Fig. 5.125a

Fig. 5.125b

Fig. 5.125c

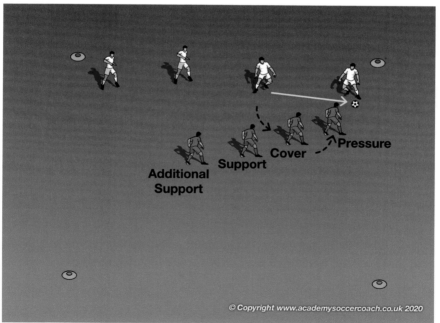

Fig. 5.125d

Drill Variations

- Attackers just play from side to side and do not try to advance the ball, making it easier for defenders to focus on sliding without also having to move upward and backward.
- The attackers play two or three touches in order to speed up the play and make the defenders transition more quickly between roles and positions.

Coaching Interventions

Problem

The defensive players do not get into the right defensive configuration based on the position of the ball.

Possible Cause #1: The defending players do not communicate and thus get confused about who is supposed to pressure the ball.

Practice Intervention: *Freeze—Demonstrate how to decisively call out "Ball!" when pressuring the ball. The pressuring defender is often the defending player directly in front of the ball. As the ball moves laterally, the pressuring defender will drop back, and a new defender will step forward and apply pressure. This switch only works with timely communication. Players should rehearse calling out "Ball!" in a strong voice. *Direct—Coach the players during the drill about who should be the one to call out and pressure the ball.

Possible Cause #2: The defending players do not mark spaces, but instead get dragged out of position while man-marking the attackers off the ball.

Practice Intervention: *Freeze—Explain to the defenders that they are marking vital spaces and should not always follow attacking players when they move away from the ball. Since the primary concern is the ball, players must stay focused to ensure that the player pressuring the ball is always covered and supported. Show defenders that following attackers and abandoning vital spaces can leave the pressuring defender isolated. *Direct—Coach the players within the game about where defenders should be positioned.

Possible Cause #3: The defending players react too slowly to the movement of the ball.

Practice Intervention: *Freeze—Demonstrate how to be "quick and decisive" when reacting to the movement of the ball. Defenders need to stay on the balls of the feet and at an angled stance to the ball in order to quickly slide side to side or up and back when the ball moves. The movement of the defenders should be in synch, and communication is key to the defensive group's moving together. *Direct—Coach players to move quickly and react faster to the movement of the ball. *Fitness—Players should do agility training to improve their ability to quickly change directions.

Competitive Game

2v2, 3v3, or 4v4 Defensive Game with End Zones—Moderate Difficulty

After learning the movement of defending in a block-zonal defense without trying to win the ball, the two sides now play a game where the goal is to pass or dribble the ball into the end zone. The defending team goes on attack after winning the ball and needs to make two passes before scoring, which gives the attacking team time to transition into the defending shape. The game is played with the offside rule, so attacking players are not allowed to make runs behind the defenders before the time of the pass (Fig. 5.126).

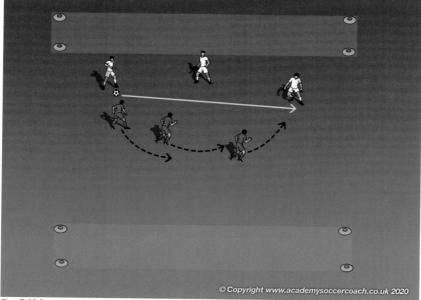

Fig. 5.126

Other Exercises

Individual Defending Techniques in an Open Area—Easy Drill

Players play in a large area. Half the players start with the ball. Players with a ball pass it to other players in the group who do not have a ball, then perform a defending technique on the players receiving the pass. Each player who receives the ball passes to a new player who does not have a ball and performs the same defensive skill. Alternate defensive techniques every few minutes (Fig. 5.127).

Fig. 5.127

1v1 Pressure (A)

After a pass, the player runs after the ball and in a defensive stance applies pressure to the receiver of the pass and shuffles backward as the player with the ball dribbles. After about five yards, the defensive player lets the attacker go. The attacker passes to another player and becomes the defender.

Block Tackle (B)

The player passes to a player without a ball, who traps the ball. The passer runs up and performs a "block tackle" on the ball, a play in which the two players aim to strike the ball at the same time. The player who received the pass then collects the ball and passes to a new player to perform the next block tackle.

Note: If the addition of space and running at the ball makes it too difficult to learn how to conduct a block tackle, players can first practice block tackling by standing across from each other with a ball between them. The coach can tell players when to start. Each takes a short step at the same time and then kicks at the ball. After each tackle, the ball is put back between the two players and another tackle is done. This is repeated until the players have demonstrated the ability to do a block tackle correctly. In a block tackle, the tackling foot is in the same form as in a push pass, with a very firm ankle. (A floppy ankle can lead to injuries.) The tackle is done with a short, quick, powerful thrust of the inside of the foot toward the ball, with very little follow-through of the foot.

No-Turn Pressure (C)

The player passes the ball to another player who allows the ball to go between the legs and turns and follows the pass with the back to the passer. The passer runs up and applies pressure in a defensive stance from behind. In this angled position, the defender can see the ball from one side of the dribbler while making it difficult for the player to turn around. The defender should also be trying to poke the ball away from the receiver through the legs. After a few yards, the defender lets the attacker go.

Slide Tackle (D)

The receiver of the pass dribbles away from the passer. The passer performs a slide tackle to knock the ball away. The player dribbling retrieves the ball, passes to another player, then performs the slide tackle.

Note: Most players will want to be trained in slide tackles before doing them with a player dribbling the ball. It is usually better to learn slide tackling on a wet day or with plastic sweatpants so that the player slides better and does not get a painful turf burn. Slide tackling is an advanced technique.

Phase of Play	Defending
Coaching Element	#10 Block-Zonal Defending
Development Stage	II Competitive Game
Drill	"2v2, 3v3, or 4v4 Transition Defensive End Zone Game"

Learning Objective

Players will learn how to defend in a block-zonal formation in a competitive transition game.

Drill Description

Three teams of two to four players compete. Goals are scored by dribbling into the end zone or passing to someone running into the end zone. One team starts with the ball and one team defends. A third team waits to rotate into the game. After the attacking team scores or loses the ball, the defending team goes off, the attackers become the defenders, and the team that was off becomes the attacking team. Play with the offside rule. The new attacking team must make two passes before they can score (Fig. 5.128).

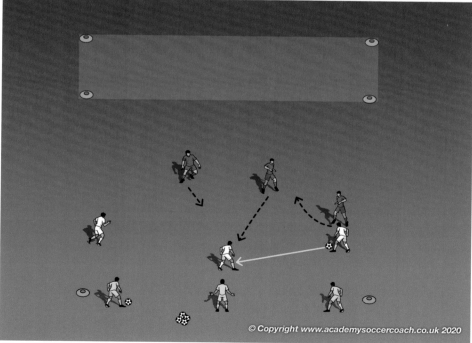

Fig. 5.128

Player Principles

10.5 Defenders who pressure the ball need to "drop back immediately after the attacker passes the ball" in order to fill in the space behind them and provide cover or support (Fig. 5.129a).

Fig. 5.129a

Defenders often make the mistake of following the ball rather than filling spaces behind them. It is common for defenders to make their first step toward the person receiving the ball rather than taking a step backward. When a player does not step back immediately, the attacking team can exploit the space behind the defender with a wall pass (Fig. 5.129b).

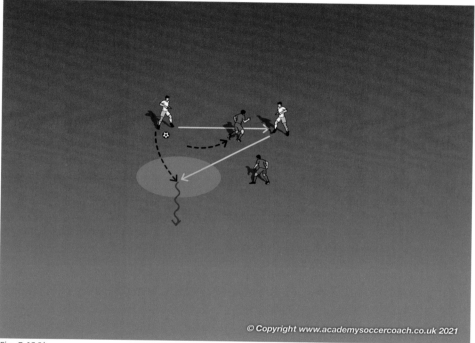

Fig. 5.129b

10.6 Until the ball is passed, a defender "should not give up pressuring the ball" until called off by another defender.

A defender who pressures an attacker on the ball should not stop pressuring until another player calls the defender off. It can be confusing for the defense if attackers dribble laterally across the field in front of the defense or if attackers perform an overlap by running around the player on the ball. If the player pressuring the ball assumes that another player will take over pressuring the attacker and drops off before the covering player can step forward, the attacker could be left with a wide-open shot on goal or the chance to pass forward.

As the overlapping player moves around the player with the ball, the supporting player needs to call the pressuring player off the ball, which allows the pressuring player to track the overlapping player (Fig. 5.130a).

Fig. 5.130a

Similarly, when an attacker dribbles laterally across the field, the covering defender can call off the pressing defender when the dribbler enters the covering defender's zone (Fig. 5.130b).

Fig. 5.130b

10.7 Defenders should not tackle the ball unless they are "100% certain of winning the ball."

A good dribbler can easily dribble past a defender who overcommits. Defenders must be patient while defending and not jab at the ball as soon as they are within kicking distance of the ball. A defender's tackle is typically done with a block tackle with the inside of the foot, or a toe poke. Defenders should be careful not to kick the ball off the attacker's shins, which can result in the ball bouncing behind the defender toward the goal.

Drill Progression

1. 2v2v2
2. 3v3v3
3. 4v4v4

Drill Variations

- The field can be made wider to make defending harder, or narrower to make defending easier.
- Encourage the attacking team to perform actions like an overlap or switching sides of the field that challenge the defenders.

Coaching Interventions

Problem #1
The attacking team is able to dribble past the defenders into the end zone.

Possible Cause #1: The defenders do not pressure the ball correctly.

Practice Intervention: *Demonstrate—Between games, show the proper angled stance to pressure the ball, about arm's length from the attacker, with active feet. It is very important that the defender does not jab at the ball, but is patient and waits for the right time to tackle the ball. *Direct—Coach the players in the game how to pressure the player on the ball without getting so close that it would be easy to dribble past them. There are usually specific players who will need repeated reminders not to jab at the ball.

Possible Cause #2: The defenders do not cover and support the ball correctly.

Practice Intervention: *Demonstrate—Between games, show players the defensive movements to use when attackers pass the ball side to side. Defenders need to anticipate where to run and get into the right positions to offer pressure, cover, and support. Players must find the right angles where they are near enough to offer a player support without being so close that they cannot cover vital passing lanes. *Direct—Coach the players in the game how to properly cover and support the defender pressuring the ball.

Problem #2

The attacking team is able to pass around and through the defenders to score.

Possible Cause #1: The covering and supporting defenders are positioned in a straight line.

Practice Intervention: *Direct—Tell players how being in a straight line can lead to easier opportunities for attackers to make through balls. Coach the defenders in the game to provide angular cover and support that can block passing lanes and allow defenders to better recover if a through ball is made.

Possible Cause #2: The defenders do not shift fast enough when the ball is passed from side to side, allowing attackers to get around the sides of the defense.

Practice Intervention: *Direct—Even when the primary focus is the attacker on the ball, defenders must be aware of the positioning of players off the ball. Defenders need to quickly move as a group when the attackers switch the point of attack. Coach the players to anticipate passes in order to react quickly.

Other Exercises

2v2, 3v3, or 4v4 Defensive End Zone Game with Goalkeepers—Moderate Difficulty

Players play in groups that form one defensive line. Players can pass to their goalkeeper in the end zone in order to help keep possession (Fig. 5.131). The goalkeeper should be actively directing the defenders about which adjustments they should make when defending.

Note: In these drills, it can be helpful for the coach to stand behind one of the defensive units to best see and encourage the movements of the defenders in relation to the movements of the ball and attackers. Later, the role of the coach can be taken over by a goalkeeper.

© Copyright www.academysoccercoach.co.uk 2020

Fig. 5.131

1v1, 2v2, 3v3, or 4v4 (+GKs) Small-Sided Shot-Blocking Game—Moderate Difficulty

Two teams compete on a small field to score on standard goals. A point is earned for either scoring a goal or blocking a shot on goal.

4v4+4 Passing Across a Defensive Zone—Advanced Drill

Four players line up on either side of a defensive zone where four other players are positioned. The four players in the center zone cannot leave the marked-out area. The four players on either side of the center zone pass the ball back and forth and attempt to pass the ball across the center zone. The team of four that can pass through the four defenders gets a point. The defending team can move out of the defensive zone when it blocks a pass from one side to the other (Fig. 5.132).

Fig. 5.132

Phase of Play	Defending
Coaching Element	#10 Block-Zonal Defending
Development Stage	III Positional Game
Drill	"8v8 Defensive Game With a Standard Goal"

Learning Objective

Players will learn how to defend in two lines in a block-zonal defense in a game-like environment.

Drill Description

8v8

Attacking Team: 2-3-3

Defending Team: 4-3+GK.

The attacking team scores on the standard goal. When the ball goes out of play, the ball restarts with the attacking team. The defense scores by passing through the small goals (Fig. 5.133).

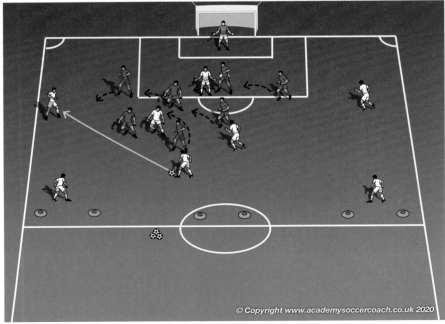

Fig. 5.133

Player Principles

10.8 The two lines of defense must "move together."

As the ball moves vertically and laterally, the two lines of defense should move in sync with one another (Fig. 5.134*a*).

Fig. 5.134a

The two defensive lines should stay compact and proportional to each other in their positioning. Staying compact reduces the space between the defensive lines where attacking players can check to receive a pass (Fig. 5.134b).

Fig. 5.134b

10.9 Defenders need to "adjust" their positions as the attacking play changes, stepping up when the ball is passed away from the goal and dropping off when a through ball is possible.

When attackers play the ball away from the goal, the defense has the opportunity to push their lines up and pressure the space around the attackers who are farther away from the goal (Fig. 5.135).

Fig. 5.135

The defense should drop off and run back toward their goal when an attacker has the chance to play a through ball. The cues for a through ball are 1) the attacker has time and space to pass forward, 2) there is space behind the defense to pass into, and 3) there is an attacker who can run into the space (Fig. 5.136).

Fig. 5.136

10.10 The defense, especially the goalkeeper, should "communicate" about where the defensive line should move.

It is important that defenders and the goalkeeper talk with one another, using consistent directive terms:

"Out": The defensive line should move quickly up the field. This type of instruction is often used when the defense is able to clear the ball far upfield, allowing defenders the time and opportunity to push up away from their goal.

"Up" or "Step": The defensive line should step up a few yards.

"Drop": Typically, the defensive line should fall back toward their goal when defending a potential through ball or counterattack, taking up a new defensive position near their penalty box. If they drop any farther than that, the attackers will have a close shot on goal. If they stop too high, or far from their goal, the attackers will still have an opportunity to pass a through ball behind the defense.

"Hold": This means the defenders should not move up or back but remain where they are.

"No shot": This directive from goalkeepers tells defenders to get a foot or body in front of attackers about to shoot.

"Slide left" or "Slide right": This directive tells defenders to move to the left or right as a group and is typically used when the ball is played laterally across the goal.

"Clear": This indicates that players must clear the ball away from the goal and that the goalkeeper is unable to catch, kick, or punch the ball away.

10.11 The defenders need to "block shots" without overcommitting and letting the attacker dribble past.

It is not uncommon for defenders to jump in the air, turn, and close their eyes when someone is about to shoot. All too often, this results in the attacker cutting the ball to the side and getting an easier shot on goal. The key for defending shots is to keep the feet moving, pressure the ball from the right distance (about arm's length), and lift only one foot at a time when blocking a shot. The defender must remain agile and able to change directions if the attacker fakes the shot and attempts to dribble.

10.12 The defenders need to "clear the ball high, wide and far."

If the ball must be cleared away from the goal, defenders need to balance power and safety. Swinging too hard could result in the player missing the ball, while kicking the ball too softly could mean it does not go far enough away from the goal.

Drill Progression

1. Initially, the attackers should start with the ball in the attacking half and with the defenders already lined up in two lines of defense in front of the goal. The focus is on lateral movements—sliding back and forth in front of the goal.
2. Next, the attackers should start with the ball in their defensive half with the defensive team close to the halfway line. This will create space for attackers to run behind the defense, challenging defenders to choose when to hold their line and when to drop off as the focus on vertical movement is added to the game.

Coaching Interventions

Problem #1

The attacking team is able to pass the ball through the defensive lines to create scoring opportunities.

Possible Cause: The defensive lines are too far apart, leaving gaps where the attackers can receive the ball "between the lines."

Practice Intervention: *Freeze—Stop the game and show the players how the defensive lines have to stay compact and connected, say, 10 to 15 yards apart. *Explain—Discuss at restarts how well players are organizing defensive lines. *Direct—Coach the defensive lines in the game to stay close together.

Problem #2

The attacking team creates shots on goal.

Possible Cause: The defending players do not block shots.

Practice Intervention: *Freeze—Stop the game and show the defenders how to keep their feet active when applying pressure to the ball and how to block a shot without jumping and overcommitting. Encourage the goalkeeper to alert defenders when to block shots when attackers are about to shoot. *Direct—When attackers have the ball in front of the goal, coach the defense when to focus on shot-blocking.

Problem #3

The defending team is unable to clear the ball.

Possible Cause #1: The defenders are not active and aggressive enough when the ball is played into the penalty box.

Practice Intervention: *Direct—Coach players who are slow to react to "be alert" and "be alive" when a ball is played into the dangerous areas.

Possible Cause #2: After winning the ball, the defenders make the wrong decision regarding when to keep possession and when to clear the ball.

Practice Intervention: *Freeze—Stop the game and explain the type of situations in which the ball should be cleared—for example, lots of pressure, no place to play, and possession directly in front of the goal. Reiterate these points during restarts.

Other Exercises

6v6 Defensive Game with an End Zone—Moderate Difficulty

The attacking team in a 3-3 formation tries to score by dribbling or passing into the end zone against the defending team in a 4-2 formation. The defending team scores by passing the ball through the small goals. Play with the offside rule.

Drill Variation

- More players can be added to each team to make the game more complex.

Phase of Play	Defending
Coaching Element	#10 Block-Zonal Defending
Development Stage	IV Standard Game
Drill	"11v11"

Learning Objective

The players will learn how to defend in a 4-4-2 or 4-5-1 formation in a standard game.

Drill Description

4-3-3 v 4-3-3

Both teams will attack in a 4-3-3 formation while defending in a 4-4-2 formation. Teams will not press each other, but will drop back into a block-zonal formation after losing the ball. The teams can also defend in a 4-5-1 formation by having both wing forwards drop back into the midfield when the ball is lost.

Player Principles

10.13 Players "interchange positions" to create two defensive lines of four.

Teams playing in a 4-3-3 create two banks of four when defending, with the wing forward farthest from the ball dropping into the midfield. Once the defending team wins the ball, then the player returns to the wide forward position (Fig. 5.137a).

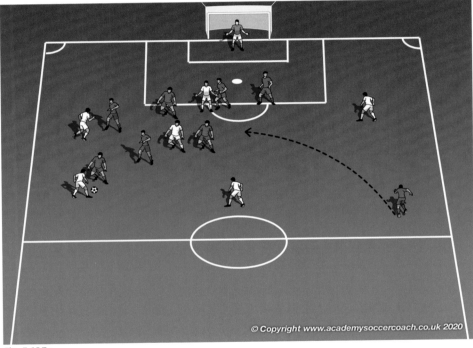

Fig. 5.137a

For more defensive protection, teams playing in a 4-3-3 can also shift into a 4-5-1 formation (or 4-1-4-1) by dropping both wing forwards back into the midfield (Fig. 5.137*b*).

Fig. 5.137b

10.14 The defensive players need to "double up in deep, wide areas" to stop crosses.

Teams need a strategy to defend crosses. The field is too wide for players to stay compact in a block-zonal defensive shape if the ball goes deep and wide.

One solution is to leave the forward 1v1 with the outside fullback while the remaining defenders slide toward the center of the goal where the cross will arrive (Fig. 5.138a). In this scenario, where there is so much room to dribble, the attacker often has the advantage and frequently can find a way to cross the ball.

Fig. 5.138a

It can be difficult for a midfielder to provide the double team on the outside because there are no designated outside midfielders in a 4-3-3. It is also a long run for the outside forward, who has to return to a defensive position and still have the energy to attack once the team has won the ball.

A second option is for a center fullback to slide outside to provide the pressuring defender support. The remaining two defenders stay in the center of the goal and are helped by the defensive center midfielder who drops back to fill in for the center back (Fig. 5.138b). In this double interchange of positions, the defending team is only moving players one position over (center defensive midfielder drops back, the center fullback slides wide) and not two (center midfielder sliding over and dropping back, or the forward coming back into the defensive line). In the double interchange, the outside fullback can pressure the wide forward with defensive support, making it much more difficult for the opponent's forward to get off an uncontested cross while the goal area remains covered with a minimum of three defenders.

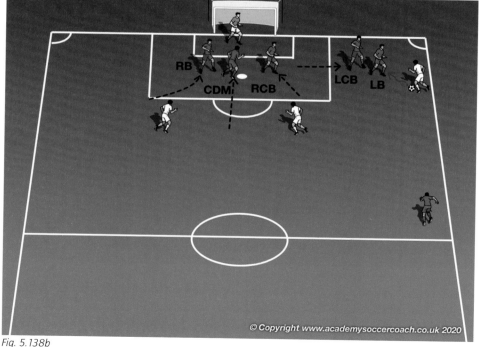

Fig. 5.138b

Coaching Interventions

Problem

The team gives up quick attacking chances after losing the ball.

Possible Cause: The team is unable to transition quickly into a block-zonal formation after losing the ball.

Practice Intervention: *Freeze—Players can be slow to transition to two lines of block-zonal defending after being spread out in an attacking shape. Show how the player nearest to the ball should apply pressure to give the remaining players time to move into covering and supportive positions. *Direct—Coach players to apply pressure in the game and to drop into a block-zonal formation.

Alternative Formations

9v9 Formation
3-2-3 v 3-2-3

Teams defend in a 3-3-2 formation with a wing forward dropping back into the midfield when defending.

7v7 Formation
3-1-2 v 3-1-2

By having one forward drop back into the midfield, teams will defend in a 3-2-1 formation.

5v5 Formation
2-1-1 v 2-1-1

Teams defend in a 2-2 formation by having the forward drop back into the midfield.

COACHING ELEMENT #11 PRESSING

Andres Iniesta and Spanish teammates press the opponent with the ball.

Phase of Play	Defending
Coaching Element	#11 Pressing
Development Stage	I Skills and Tactics
Drill	"Agility Drills"

Learning Objective

Players will improve their agility needed to press.

Drill Description

Half the players have a ball, half do not. Players move and pass to each other in a designated area with cones. On the coach's command, players perform agility drills before returning to passing the balls among themselves (Fig. 5.139).

Fig. 5.139

Player Principles

11.1 Players must "react quickly" to changes in the game.

Mental quickness is key to pressing. Players need to press quickly after losing the ball, before the opponent has had a chance to regroup.

11.2 Players must "make sharp turns" when changing directions.

Players need to turn sharply and quickly when changing directions. They should brake with the inside foot before exploding in the new direction with the outside foot.

Skills Introduced

Agility

- Stopping
- Changing directions
- Jumping and landing
- Quick starts

Drill Progression

1. While players are passing the balls within the group, the coach shouts out an agility drill to do before players return to passing the ball. There are many drill options: touch three cones, shuffle between three cones, run backward between three cones, or do a jumping head ball at three cones, etc.

2. To keep players more engaged, vary the passing drills between agility drills. For example, players can practice two-touch passing, combination passing, wall passing, and through balls to reinforce essential skills.

Coaching Interventions

Problem #1

Players do not cut quickly when changing directions.

Possible Cause: When turning at the cone, players are braking with the foot closest to the cone.

Practice Intervention: *Freeze—Demonstrate how to 1) slow down and stop with small steps, 2) use the leg furthest from the cone to slow momentum with the knees bent before coming to a stop, and 3) use the leg closest to the cone to explode to the opposite side. *Direct—Coach players in the drill how to change directions correctly. *Drill Change—Players who continue to lunge at cones with straight legs should practice slowly until they turn correctly.

Problem #2

The players sprint too slowly.

Possible Cause: Players run on their heels, with their toes pointed outward or inward, with straight arms or without lifting their knees.

Practice Intervention: *Freeze—Players need to be shown proper running/sprinting technique: feet pointed forward, arms bent at 90 degrees, high knees, sprinting on the balls of the feet. *Direct—Coach players to use good running form when sprinting.

Competitive Game

Agility Relay Race—Easy Drill

Without soccer balls, groups of players compete doing a series of agility drills which include changes in direction, jumping, backward running, and shuttle runs (Fig. 5.140).

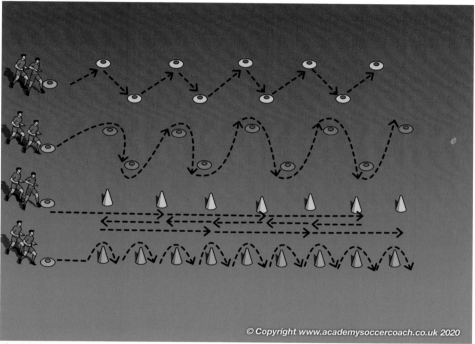

Fig. 5.140

Phase of Play	Defending
Coaching Element	#11 Pressing
Development Stage	II Competitive Game
Drill	"5v3 Defensive Pressing Game"

Learning Objective

Players will learn how to press together to win the ball back.

Drill Description

5v3

Five players play keep-away against three defenders in a designated area. The three defenders work together by pressing the attackers in order to win the ball and then make two passes for a point. Attackers score by making seven passes in a row. The five attackers press the ball after they lose possession and try to win the ball back in three seconds (Fig. 5.141).

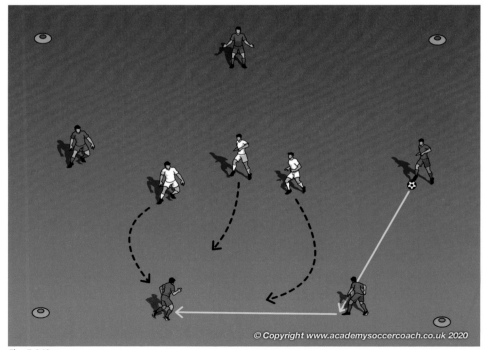

Fig. 5.141

Player Principles

11.3 Press the ball to "cut out passing lanes" and "force attackers toward support."

The pressing players need to curl their runs toward the player on the ball to cut out easy passing options, in order to make the attackers' play more predictable and improve chances of winning the ball (Fig. 5.141).

11.4 The defenders need to "press together" to win the ball back.

Players need to learn how to hunt down the ball in packs. A single player will waste energy trying to chase the ball alone.

Coaching Interventions

Problem

The three defensive players do not win the ball back.

Possible Cause #1: Players are not working together to press.

Practice Intervention: *Demonstrate—Between games, explain to players how to press the ball as a group with curled runs to cut out passing lanes. Players need to be aware of each other's movements. *Direct—Coach specific players pressuring the ball where they can run to cut out passing lanes.

Possible Cause #2: Players are not working hard to get the ball back.

Practice Intervention: *Explanation—Between games, discuss with players the high energy required to pressure the ball and cut out passing angles. *Drill Change—Provide more rest for players so they can always run at 100%.

Other Exercise

7v4 Pressing Game with Defensive Limitations—Moderate Difficulty

There are six attackers around the edge of the marked-out area and one attacker in the middle. Mark out a diamond in the center of the field. At any one time, only three defenders can press the ball outside of the diamond. This encourages defenders to communicate with each other about who is pressing the ball (Fig. 5.142).

© Copyright www.academysoccercoach.co.uk 2020

Fig. 5.142

Phase of Play	Defending
Coaching Element	#11 Pressing
Development Stage	III Positional Game
Drill	"8v8 Positional Pressing Game to a Standard Game"

Learning Objective

Players will learn how to win the ball back quickly after losing possession in their attacking half.

Drill Description

8v8

Attacking Team: 2-3-3

Defending Team: 4-3+GK

The attacking team starts with the ball and can score on the goal after they make five consecutive passes, which encourages creating Rondo formations. Attackers try to win the ball back within five seconds after they lose possession. The defense earns a point by scoring in small goals at the halfway line (Fig. 5.143).

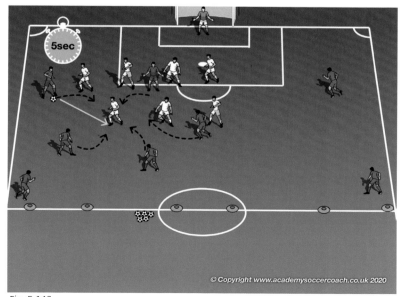

Fig. 5.143

Player Principle

11.5 The attacking players need to "press as a team" to win the ball back quickly.

The attacking team is pressing from specific positions now, which affects how they pressure the ball together. The pressing should be intense but organized and structured around a player's position on the field.

Coaching Interventions

Problem

The attacking team does not win the ball back after losing possession.

Possible Cause: The attacking players are too spread out to effectively press the opponent when the attackers lose the ball.

Practice Intervention: *Freeze—Stop the game and show players how probing in the attacking half in a Rondo formation sets up the attacking team to better press the opponent after they lose possession. *Direct—Coach specific players how to get numbers around the ball to help keep possession in the attacking third and to be in a good place to press when the ball is lost.

Other Exercises

6v6 Pressing End Zone Game—Moderate Difficulty

The attacking team plays in a 3-3 formation against the defensive team, which is in a 4-2 formation. The attacking team scores by dribbling the ball into the end zone after completing four consecutive passes. The defensive team scores by passing the ball through small goals. The requirement to complete four consecutive passes encourages the attacking team to create the Rondo formation around the ball, setting up the opportunity to press when they lose the ball.

Phase of Play	Defending
Coaching Element	#11 Pressing
Development Stage	IV Standard Game
Drill	"11v11"

Learning Objective

Players will improve their skill at winning the ball immediately after losing possession in the attacking half in a standard game.

Drill Description

4-3-3 v 4-3-3

Teams will attack in a 4-3-3 with a focus on pressing when the ball has been lost in the opponent's half. When unable to win the ball back by pressing, teams will defend in a 4-4-2 block-zonal formation and look to counterattack.

Player Principle

11.6 Decide "when to press and when to drop off" into a block-zonal defense.

As practice progresses to a game with two standard goals, teams need to decide when to press and try to win the ball back immediately and when to drop off and defend in a block-zonal defense.

Cues for the team to press:

1. The ball is lost in the attacking half of the field.
2. The attacking team has numbers around the ball.
3. The opponent on the ball is facing their goal.
4. The opponent on the ball does not have full control of the ball.

Cues for the team to drop off into a defensive block:

1. The ball is lost in the team's defensive half.
2. The opponent on the ball has the ball under control, with space and time to look up and potentially pass forward.
3. The team does not have numbers around the ball.

Coaching Interventions

Problem

The attacking team gives up easy scoring opportunities after losing possession of the ball.

Possible Cause: The attacking team is making the wrong decision as to when to press and when to drop off in a block defense, leaving the team vulnerable to counterattacks.

Practice Intervention: *Freeze—Stop the game and show the players the situations in which they should press or drop off. Review the cues to press or drop off. *Direct—Coach players in the game when they should press or drop off in a block-zonal formation.

Alternative Formations

9v9 Formation
3-2-3 v 3-2-3

The teams attack in a 3-2-3 with a focus on probing and pressing, while defending in a 3-3-2 to improve block-zonal defending and counterattacking.

7v7 Formation
2-3-1 v 2-3-1

The team attacks in a 2-3-1 and defends in a 3-2-1 with a midfielder dropping back into the defensive line.

5v5 Formation
1-2-1 v 1-2-1

In attack, the team will play in a 1-2-1, while defending in a 2-2.

CHAPTER 6

PRACTICE PLANNING: USING PRACTICE MODULES TO DESIGN YOUR SEASON-LONG TRAINING PLAN

"A stable and high performance level can only be achieved through long-term training design."

(Jankowski 2016, pg. 39)

Coaches who don't plan should not plan to coach, since the process of developing a team's game model will take much thought. Over the course of the season, the goal is for your team to be competent in using all styles of play equally well. A practice that does not fit within an overall training plan will be much less effective. The goal of each practice is to incorporate new concepts into the team's play while consolidating previously learned skills and tactics. Team practices are not isolated events, but build on each other throughout the season.

THE PRACTICE PLAN "HEAT MAPS"

The training plan displayed here uses 10 practice modules to teach the 11 coaching elements during a soccer season. The amount of time required for each module can vary from one practice session to several weeks, depending on your team's needs and the length of your season. It is recommended that you introduce all the coaching elements, regardless of your players' inexperience or the shortness of your season, to ensure that your players are introduced to the essential skills and tactics of soccer.

Soccer is not a sport where players train for a final event. A team needs to be prepared to play a weekly game. Even though specific coaching elements are learned progressively throughout the season, players are exposed to all the game elements during the warm-up and standard games at every practice. For more advanced teams, tactical learning can occur mostly in the preseason, since they will need fine-tuning rather than deep learning.

The team rating form provided in the appendix will allow you to monitor your team's progress incorporating the coaching elements in their play. The rating form will be useful for a director of coaching, who can monitor the progress of several teams by requesting that the team coaches turn in a copy of their practice plans and rating forms from each practice. When teams appear to be stalled in their development, the coaching director can review the coaches' team-rating forms and the practice plans to determine the possible reasons for the teams' lack of growth.

Introducing too much new information at once can overwhelm a player; conversely, not introducing enough new learning can lead to boredom. An essential art of coaching is finding a balance between teaching new skills and tactics and rehearsing previously learned material.

DRAWING UP A PRACTICE PLAN

Think outside of the box (Fig. 6.1).

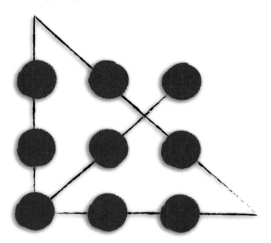

Fig. 6.1

To create a well-thought-out practice plan, start with several sheets of paper on which you can display the player principles, drill descriptions, diagrams, sketches, and other important notes. Do not limit yourself to one side of a sheet of paper with pre-drawn boxes for all of your practice ideas. The more details you add to the plan, the better you will be able to coach the practice. Take time to visualize how you will coach each drill and the transition between drills, to "see" how well the exercises will work out with spacing, numbers, and scoring systems.

Incorporate fitness training into a team practice by adjusting the intensity, duration and spacing of a drill. Agility training can introduce, improve, and reinforce the movements and skills required in that particular practice. Sprint training should be included in most practices to improve player speed.

ECONOMICAL COACHING APPROACHES

Because time is a limiting component at every practice, be economical in how you coach.

1. Your team should practice as they intend to play. Drills should include technical, tactical, fitness, and psychological components so the learning can be effectively generalized to the game environment.

2. Drills should not always just focus on improving either the defense or the offense. For example, in a practice focused on 1v1 dribbling, have a second coach teach defending techniques to the players when they are in a defensive role.

3. Leave out of your practice plan what the team has already learned. For example, if a team is focused on learning the coaching element of probing passing and the players are already skilled at Rondo passing drills, then skip the Stage 1 skill development and focus on teaching Rondo passing in the competitive and positional games of Stages 2 and 3.

4. Organize activities so players are always engaged during drills. Ensure that the time between drills is kept to a minimum. Drills should be described succinctly. Long-winded explanations will not improve the quality of the practice. It is better to start a drill with a few players still confused than to spend extra time ensuring all players understand the drill perfectly, since some players will only understand the exercise once they start doing it.

5. Be creative about when to teach a soccer lesson or skill. For example, the warm-up time before a game can be used to teach or improve a skill or tactic. Learning something new prior to a game can also sharpen the players' minds and excite them for the game.

A SEASON-LONG TRAINING PLAN

PRACTICE MODULE 1

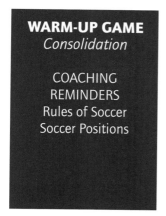

WARM-UP GAME
Consolidation

COACHING
REMINDERS
Rules of Soccer
Soccer Positions

**SKILL AND
TACTICAL
DEVELOPMENT**
Acquisition

ELEMENT 1
Passing Around Light
Pressure
Stages 1,2,3

**STANDARD
GAME**
Incorporation

COACHING
EMPHASIS
Passing Around Light
Pressure

COACHING
REMINDERS
Rules of Soccer
Soccer Positions

In practice Module 1, focus on the skills and tactics utilized to build up out of the back under light pressure. In the standard game, remind defenders to get wide and deep when the goalkeeper has the ball. In this position, the defender is open to the field and can receive the ball with the second foot to easily change the direction of play. Players should also be encouraged to turn away from pressure and pass back to support, rather than force the ball up the field.

PRACTICE MODULE 2

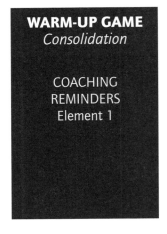

WARM-UP GAME
Consolidation

COACHING
REMINDERS
Element 1

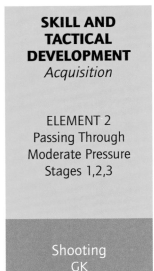

**SKILL AND
TACTICAL
DEVELOPMENT**
Acquisition

ELEMENT 2
Passing Through
Moderate Pressure
Stages 1,2,3

Shooting
GK

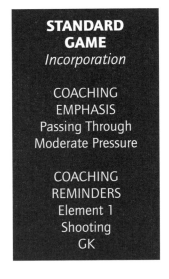

**STANDARD
GAME**
Incorporation

COACHING
EMPHASIS
Passing Through
Moderate Pressure

COACHING
REMINDERS
Element 1
Shooting
GK

In the warm-up game, remind players about the importance of playing away from pressure.

In the skill and tactical development stages in Module 2, teach players to build up out of the back by creating space, making timed checks to the ball, and receiving the ball with a protected half-turn to face upfield when under moderate pressure. You should also instruct players to use verbal and nonverbal communication skills to improve team passing.

In this module, you begin to weave in attacking skills such as shooting. Attacking skills are challenging to learn and need time to master, so they should be introduced early in the season and reviewed frequently.

With the introduction of shooting, the coach can begin to work more with goalkeepers. Since many drills involve shooting, it is not always necessary for you to organize goalkeeper practices separate from the team practice. During drills not involving shooting, your goalkeepers can join the field players in practicing foot skills, an important requirement in the modern game where goalkeepers can play as much with their feet as with their hands.

In the standard game, you should focus on ensuring players utilize coaching element #2 ideas in the game, while also remembering the important skills and tactics from coaching element #1 (making space, receiving with the second foot, and offering deep angles of support). Discuss proper shooting technique without taking too much time away from the emphasis of this practice period: learning how to pass through moderate pressure.

PRACTICE MODULE 3

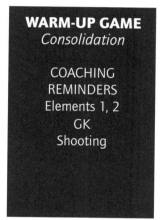

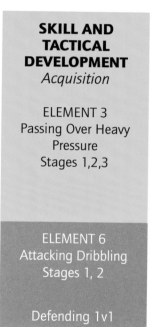

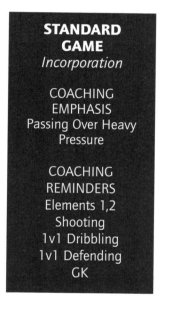

In the warm-up game, remind players about the essential coaching points from coaching elements #1 and #2, such as making the field large when the goalkeeper has the ball, providing support through deep angles, checking to the ball, and receiving the ball with protected half-turns.

In Module 3, players focus on learning how to bring the ball out of the defensive half by passing directly over the opponents' heavy pressure, using long passes from the defenders to the forwards. The skills and tactics introduced include passing and trapping a long, lofted ball and providing support for knockdowns.

As shooting skills improve, 1v1 dribbling moves are introduced, first without pressure from a defender and then with defensive pressure. Players practice shooting on goal after doing a dribbling move. Players learn 1v1 defending skills.

In the standard game, all the build-up elements are coached, with particular emphasis on playing over the opponent's heavy pressure. At appropriate times, also coach players how to dribble and shoot correctly.

PRACTICE MODULE 4

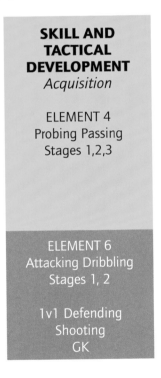

WARM-UP GAME
Consolidation

COACHING
REMINDERS
Phase 1
GK
Shooting
1v1 Dribbling
1v1 Defending

SKILL AND TACTICAL DEVELOPMENT
Acquisition

ELEMENT 4
Probing Passing
Stages 1,2,3

ELEMENT 6
Attacking Dribbling
Stages 1, 2

1v1 Defending
Shooting
GK

STANDARD GAME
Incorporation

COACHING
EMPHASIS
Probing Passing

COACHING
REMINDERS
Phase 1
Shooting
1v1 Dribbling
1v1 Defending
GK

In the warm-up game, your team should be reminded how to bring the ball out of the defensive half in three different ways (Phase 1), depending on the pressure put on the defenders by the opposing team. Players should also be encouraged to correctly shoot, dribble 1v1, and defend 1v1.

In Module 4, the skill and tactic development stages focus on ways to keep possession of the ball in the opposing team's half while looking to create opportunities to score on goal. Probing passing tactics require players to group around the ball in the opponent's half and slide in and out of tight spaces to find channels to receive passes. At least one player stays in a wide position to provide an outlet where an attack can begin away from defensive pressure.

The team should continue to advance dribbling and shooting skills.

In the standard game, you need to emphasize probing for attacking chances on goal, while also ensuring that players remember build-up tactics along with the attacking skills of shooting and dribbling. This will be the first time that you may see the successful execution of the three phases of play while in possession: build up, probing, and attack. Although build up can lead directly to an attack, now players need to start recognizing that if an attack is not immediately possible, then another option exists: probing with short passes until a chance to attack is created.

PRACTICE MODULE 5

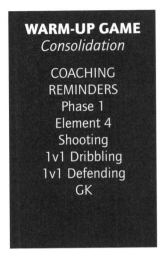

WARM-UP GAME
Consolidation

COACHING
REMINDERS
Phase 1
Element 4
Shooting
1v1 Dribbling
1v1 Defending
GK

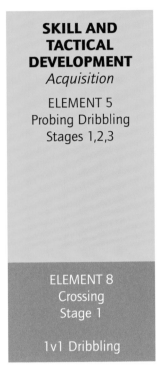

**SKILL AND
TACTICAL
DEVELOPMENT**
Acquisition

ELEMENT 5
Probing Dribbling
Stages 1,2,3

ELEMENT 8
Crossing
Stage 1

1v1 Dribbling

**STANDARD
GAME**
Incorporation

COACHING
EMPHASIS
Probing Dribbling
Probing Passing

COACHING
REMINDERS
Phase 1
Shooting
1v1 Dribbling
1v1 Defending
Crossing
GK

In the warm-up game, coach your team to build up (passing the ball out of the defensive half), probe (keeping possession with short passes in the opponent's half), attack (creating chances on goal through 1v1 dribbling and shooting), and defend (1v1).

In the skill and tactical development stages of Module 5, your team will learn probing dribbling, which includes how to dribble in tight areas and turn quickly and deceptively in a variety of ways, using more advanced skills such as the Cruyff, step-over, outside-of-the-foot, and the Xavi pirouette turn. These development stages will improve your players' abilities to create space for attacking plays.

This practice module also introduces crossing and finishing techniques. In the standard game, the coaching focus is on probing dribbling, with strong reminders about probing passing tactics which are essential for setting up players to do a turn that can free them to initiate an attack.

386

PRACTICE MODULE 6

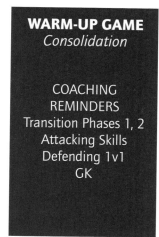

WARM-UP GAME
Consolidation

COACHING
REMINDERS
Transition Phases 1, 2
Attacking Skills
Defending 1v1
GK

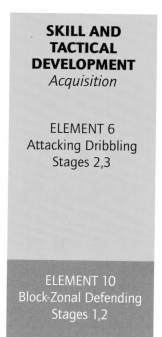

**SKILL AND
TACTICAL
DEVELOPMENT**
Acquisition

ELEMENT 6
Attacking Dribbling
Stages 2,3

ELEMENT 10
Block-Zonal Defending
Stages 1,2

**STANDARD
GAME**
Incorporation

COACHING
EMPHASIS
Attacking Dribbling
Block-Zonal Defending

COACHING
REMINDERS
Transition Phases 1,2
Attacking Skills
GK

In the warm-up game, emphasize how the team transitions from build-up (Phase 1) to probing (Phase 2) if a direct attack on goal is not possible. Attacking skills (1v1 dribbling, shooting, crossing) and 1v1 defending should also be emphasized. In Module 6, the skill and tactical development stages now focus on attacking techniques and tactics. Since dribbling moves have been practiced prior to this period, the Stage 1 drills could be skipped so the bulk of your time can be spent doing competitive and positional games.

Since attacking is now the focus, start introducing block-zonal defending tactics into practices in a more formal fashion. It is advisable to have one coach work with the attacking side and another work with the defenders. You should also set aside a separate time when the entire team can focus solely on defending. In the standard game, the focus of coaching is on helping players identify when to go 1v1 to create goal-scoring chances, correcting their technique and decision-making if attackers fail to dribble past defenders. Be sure that block-zonal defending tactics are incorporated into the game. 1v1 defending is now coached within block-zonal tactics.

PRACTICE MODULE 7

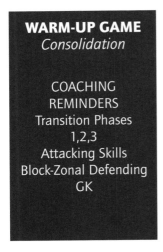

WARM-UP GAME
Consolidation

COACHING
REMINDERS
Transition Phases
1,2,3
Attacking Skills
Block-Zonal Defending
GK

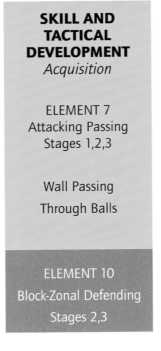

SKILL AND TACTICAL DEVELOPMENT
Acquisition

ELEMENT 7
Attacking Passing
Stages 1,2,3

Wall Passing

Through Balls

ELEMENT 10
Block-Zonal Defending
Stages 2,3

STANDARD GAME
Incorporation

COACHING
EMPHASIS
Attacking Passing
Block-Zonal Defending

COACHING
REMINDERS
Transition Phases
1,2,3
Attacking Skills
GK

In the warm-up game, reinforce your team's ability to transition between the phases of play: build-up (Phase 1), probing (Phase 2), and attacking (Phase 3).

In the skill and tactical development stages of Module 7, focus on improving your team's ability to use passing plays to create goal-scoring opportunities. Initially, your team should learn how to do wall passes separately from how to pass the ball through or over the defense.

If you combine wall passing with through balls in a drill before players can do each one competently, players will tend to do one more than the other. Once players can perform each type of passing separately, then wall passing and through balls can be combined in a single drill, say, where teams can score points for both a wall pass and a through ball.

Continue to teach block-zonal defending tactics. In the defensive practices, you should instruct how to defend through balls and wall passes. Show players when to drop off and cover the space behind them.

PRACTICE MODULE 8

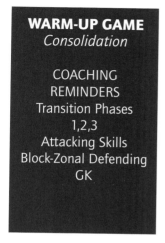

WARM-UP GAME
Consolidation

COACHING
REMINDERS
Transition Phases
1,2,3
Attacking Skills
Block-Zonal Defending
GK

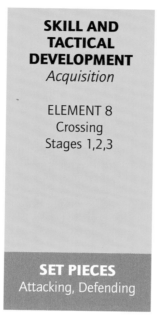

**SKILL AND
TACTICAL
DEVELOPMENT**
Acquisition

ELEMENT 8
Crossing
Stages 1,2,3

SET PIECES
Attacking, Defending

**STANDARD
GAME**
Incorporation

COACHING
EMPHASIS
Crossing
Set Pieces

COACHING
REMINDERS
Transition Phases
1,2,3
Block-Zonal Defending
Attacking Skills
GK

The movement from one phase of play to the next should become more fluid. Remind your team to quickly transition into a block-zonal defense after losing the ball.

In the skill and tactical developmental stages of Module 8, the focus is on teaching crossing techniques and tactics. Crossing opportunities will typically occur after 1v1 dribbling, passing combinations, or through balls. Your players should learn both the proper technique of crossing and finishing and how to make timed runs that free them from the defenders in front of the goal.

Free kicks can also be taught in this module, since there is much overlap between the skills and tactics of crossing and set pieces.

In the standard game, the use of crosses should be consolidated with other attacking skills and tactics to create goal-scoring chances. Arbitrary fouls can be called to provide opportunities to reinforce the skills and tactics of doing free kicks.

PRACTICE MODULE 9

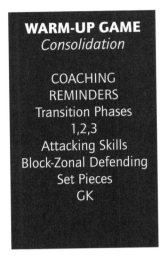

WARM-UP GAME
Consolidation

COACHING
REMINDERS
Transition Phases
1,2,3
Attacking Skills
Block-Zonal Defending
Set Pieces
GK

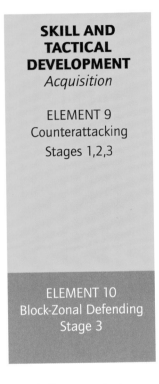

**SKILL AND
TACTICAL
DEVELOPMENT**
Acquisition

ELEMENT 9
Counterattacking
Stages 1,2,3

ELEMENT 10
Block-Zonal Defending
Stage 3

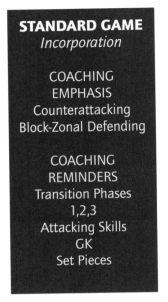

STANDARD GAME
Incorporation

COACHING
EMPHASIS
Counterattacking
Block-Zonal Defending

COACHING
REMINDERS
Transition Phases
1,2,3
Attacking Skills
GK
Set Pieces

The warm-up game should now look like your playing model, as the team can build up, probe, and attack in a variety of ways. Coach to reinforce the use of crossing to create goal-scoring chances and emphasize the quick transition to block defending when the ball is lost.

The skill and tactical development stages of Module 9 focus on the technique and tactics of counterattacking. Block-zonal defending also can be a focus, since the team practicing counterattacking can create the space to counterattack by sitting back in a deep defensive block.

Since a counterattack can start in any part of the field, your team needs to be able to identify the moments to counterattack rather than build up or probe in the standard game.

PRACTICE MODULE 10

WARM-UP GAME	SKILL AND TACTICAL DEVELOPMENT	STANDARD GAME
Consolidation	*Acquisition*	*Incorporation*
COACHING REMINDERS	ELEMENT 11	COACHING EMPHASIS
Transition Phases 1,2,3	Pressing	Pressing
Counterattacking	Stages 1,2,3	Set Pieces
Set Pieces		
GK		COACHING REMINDERS
		Transition Phases 1,2,3
		GK
	SET PIECES	
	Attacking, Defending	

In the warm-up game, remind your team when to counterattack and when to build up and probe.

In practice Module 10, coach your team to press and win the ball close to the opponent's goal in order to create quick-scoring chances. Opportunities to press can be made by bringing several players around the ball to probe in the attacking half.

The focus of the standard game is on pressing after the ball has been lost and practicing set pieces.

With the inclusion of pressing into the game model, your team now has the possibility of a "Plan A" and "Plan B." They can build up against light, moderate, and heavy pressure; maintain possession of the ball in the opponent's defensive half through short passing and creative turning; and attack the goal through combination passing, through balls, 1v1 dribbling, and crossing. The team can defend in a deep block by taking away vital areas in front of the goal and pressing high up the field to create quick chances on goal. They can also score from counterattacks and set pieces.

APPENDIX

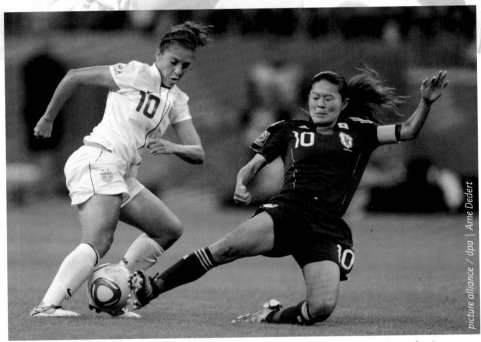

Homare Sawa of Japan tackles the ball from the US player Carli Lloyd in the World Cup final.

COACHING ELEMENTS: SKILLS AND TACTICS

ELEMENT #1

TRAPPING

- Receive with the inside of the second (outside) foot in order to switch the field
- Receive with the outside of the foot in order to switch the field

PASSING

- Push pass
- Squib pass, i.e., a long skimming pass with the instep

DRIBBLING

- Roll back

TACTICS

- The receiver drops back to receive the pass to create the best angle of support in order to trap the ball with the second foot and quickly switch the direction of play
- Players communicate in a timely manner about being open for a pass

ELEMENT #2

TRAPPING

- Half-turn (protective) across the body

PASSING

- Timed passes to the protective foot, away from defensive pressure
- One-touch passing across the body

TACTICS

- Checking away from and to the ball

ELEMENT #3

TRAPPING

- Inside-of-the-foot trap
- Outside-of-the-foot trap
- Head
- Thigh
- Chest
- Sole-of-the-foot roof trap
- Inside-of-the-foot roof trap
- Outside-of-the-foot roof trap
- Top-of-the-foot roof trap

PASSING

- Clipping/driving in the air
- Inside-of-the-foot volley pass
- Outside-of-the-foot volley pass
- Chest pass
- Head pass

ELEMENT #4

PASSING

- One- and two-touch passing under pressure

ELEMENT #5

DRIBBLING

- Roll back
- Cut
- Outside-of-the-foot turn
- Cruyff turn
- Step-over
- Roll-push
- Xavi pirouette (cut-back)
- Shielding

ELEMENT #6

DRIBBLING

- Top-of-the-foot dribbling
- Change of speed
- Fake left, go right
- Scissors
- Ronaldo Chop
- Inside-outside

FINISHING

- Instep shot

ELEMENT #7

PASSING

- Wall passes
- Combination passes
- Through balls

TACTICS

- Timed runs behind the defense
- Overlapping runs

ELEMENT #8

PASSING

- Crossing

FINISHING

- Side volley
- Inside-of-the-foot volley
- One-touch shots from crosses played on the ground
- Heading

ELEMENT #9

DRIBBLING

- Fast, straight dribbling in open space

PASSING

- Passing into the path of a sprinting player

FINISHING

- 1v1 with goalkeepers

ELEMENT #10

TACTICS

- Closing down and pressuring attackers
- Block-zonal defending shape and movements
- Tackling
- Shot and pass blocking
- Clearing the ball, defensive heading, inside-of-the-foot volley.

ELEMENT #11

AGILITY

- Stopping
- Change of directions
- Jumping and landing
- Quick starts

SUMMARY OF PLAYER PRINCIPLES

ELEMENT #1—BUILD-UP: PASSING AROUND LIGHT PRESSURE

TECHNICAL AND TACTICAL DEVELOPMENT

1.1   Players need to be in a "supportive position" to receive the pass.

1.2   Players should "receive the ball with the second (or outside) foot."

1.3   Players need to "communicate" that they are open.

COMPETITIVE GAME

1.4   Players "trap away from pressure."

1.5   Players drop off to "support the passer" with deep angles.

1.6   Players should "turn away from pressure" and not force passes through defenders.

POSITIONAL GAME

1.7   Safety v risk: Make the correct decision when to dribble and pass forward and when to pass backward.

1.8   "No square passes." Receiving players should offer angled support behind the player on the ball instead of providing support straight across or level with the passer.

STANDARD GAME

1.9 Once the team's goalkeeper collects the ball, the defenders should quickly "spread out wide and deep" to receive a pass from the goalkeeper.

1.10 The goalkeeper should "play defenders to their front" (i.e., second) foot when the defenders have space and are looking up the field in a wide position.

ELEMENT #2—BUILD-UP: PASSING THROUGH MODERATE PRESSURE

TECHNICAL AND TACTICAL DEVELOPMENT

2.1 Players need to "make space."

2.2 Players need to "create surprise" when they check.

2.3 Players need to "protect the ball" when they make the trap.

2.4 Players need to "look up" after they trap the ball in order to find the next pass.

COMPETITIVE GAME

2.5 The player receiving the pass should "trap the ball away from pressure."

2.6 Supporting players tell the receiver of the pass, "Man on" or "Turn."

2.7 The players checking to the ball should "communicate with the passer" to indicate that they want the ball passed to them at that moment.

POSITIONAL GAME

2.8   Players "communicate with the pass."

2.9   "Make the field as large as possible."

STANDARD GAME

2.10   Players need to take the initiative and check to the ball and do half-turns under moderate pressure.

ELEMENT #3—BUILD-UP: PASSING OVER HEAVY PRESSURE

TECHNICAL AND TACTICAL DEVELOPMENT

3.1   The longer, lofted pass should have a "gentle backspin on the ball."

3.2   A squib pass should "skim the surface of the ground" so the ball can travel faster over a longer distance.

3.3   The receiver of a long, lofted pass needs to "first, assess the flight of the ball; second, make a decision about how to receive it; and third, move into a position to trap the ball."

3.4   The receiver should "settle the ball to the ground" as quickly as possible after receiving the pass in the air.

COMPETITIVE GAME

3.5   Players "look for seams" to pass and receive the ball.

3.6   Players "choose the right type of pass" over longer distances.

POSITIONAL GAME

3.7   Players need to "anticipate the knockdowns" after long passes to forwards.

STANDARD GAME

3.8   Players need to learn how to "read the defense."

ELEMENT #4—PROBING: PASSING

TECHNICAL AND TACTICAL DEVELOPMENT

4.1   Passes should be "played to feet."

4.2   Receivers of the pass need to be "on their toes," ready to make quick passes.

COMPETITIVE GAME

4.3   Players need to "slide to get into supportive positions."

POSITIONAL GAME

4.4   Players need to "shift side to side" to get numbers around the ball.

4.5   "Switch the ball when you cannot go forward."

STANDARD GAME

4.6   Players need to learn when after the build up to transition to attack or to transition to probing passing.

4.7   The transition to probing passing must involve the dynamic movement of the entire team, as players quickly push up from the defense into the attacking half and assume new positions relative to the ball.

ELEMENT #5—PROBING: DRIBBLING

TECHNICAL AND TACTICAL DEVELOPMENT

5.1   Players dribble with the ball "under the body," "touching the ball every step," with the "inside and outside of the foot," and the "head up."

5.2   The dribbler needs to "turn quickly" to create space.

5.3   The players should "shield with a wide stance."

COMPETITIVE GAME

5.4   Players need to "use creative turns" to elude their marker.

POSITIONAL GAME

5.5   Players will use turns to "create attacking opportunities."

STANDARD GAME

5.6   Players will learn "when to pass and when to dribble and turn" in attacking situations.

ELEMENT #6—ATTACKING: DRIBBLING

TECHNICAL AND TACTICAL DEVELOPMENT

6.1   "Make the move early enough."

COMPETITIVE GAME

6.2   "Dribble straight at the defender" in order to "commit and engage the defender."

6.3   "Know when to pass and when to dribble."

POSITIONAL GAME

6.4   The attacking team should "find players who are 1v1."

STANDARD GAME

6.5   Players need to "take players on in the right areas of the field."

ELEMENT #7—ATTACKING: PASSING

*Wall passing and through balls should initially be coached separately, before these tactics and skills are taught together.

TECHNICAL AND TACTICAL DEVELOPMENT

7.1 The player creating the wall pass "attacks and makes the defender commit" before making the initial pass.

7.2 The cues to make a through ball are 1) "space in front of the attacker to look forward," 2) "space behind the defense to play the ball," and 3) "a player in position to make the run behind the defense."

COMPETITIVE GAME

7.3 "Provide support to the dribbler" to create wall-pass opportunities.

7.4 "Quickly get players running behind the defense" when a through pass is possible.

POSITIONAL GAME

7.5 "Create and exploit overloads."

STANDARD GAME

7.6 Players should look to exploit "third-person runs" to create attacking opportunities.

ELEMENT #8—ATTACKING: CROSSING

TECHNICAL AND TACTICAL DEVELOPMENT

8.1   The crosser should "dribble to the end line before making the cross" with the "final dribble angled toward the goal."

8.2   Crossers should "pick out the runners."

8.3   Attackers need to "leave late and arrive on time" when making runs into the box.

8.4   Runners should fill important parts of the goal area by "running to the near and far posts and the penalty spot."

8.5   Attackers need to volley hard crosses with a "big foot, not a big swing."

8.6   Players should keep the "heel over the ball" when performing a side volley.

8.7   Whenever possible, head the ball "down toward the goal line."

8.8   Crosses that cannot be shot on goal should be "redirected back to the center of the goal" for another player to finish.

COMPETITIVE GAME

8.9   Players need to "elude defenders" to get free for crosses.

POSITIONAL GAME

8.10   The attacking team can "create overloads in the channels with overlapping runs."

STANDARD GAME

8.11   Teams need to get "numbers in the box" when a crossing opportunity occurs.

ELEMENT #9—ATTACKING: COUNTERATTACKING

TECHNICAL AND TACTICAL DEVELOPMENT

9.1   Attacking players must "play quickly up the field."

9.2   Whenever possible, attacking players should "pass the ball into space" in front of teammates running forward to ensure the attacking player receiving the ball does not lose momentum.

COMPETITIVE GAME

9.3   Teams need to "quickly transition to counterattacking" when they win the ball.

9.4   As they run forward, the supporting players need to "fill gaps" between defenders to give the player on the ball passing options, to make themselves harder to mark, and to be available for through balls and early crosses.

9.5   The counterattacking player on the ball should look to "pass early" to supporting players running forward. The "ball runs faster than any player," and passing forward is quicker than a player's dribbling forward.

POSITIONAL GAME

9.6   Attacking players should take advantage of the open space and numerical advantage on the counterattack to "create high-percentage shots on goal."

STANDARD GAME

9.7   Teams need to choose whether to "build up or counterattack" when they win the ball in their defensive half.

ELEMENT #10—DEFENDING: BLOCK-ZONAL DEFENDING

TECHNICAL AND TACTICAL DEVELOPMENT

10.1   Defending players must "put pressure on the ball."

10.2   Defending players need to "provide cover for the pressure on the ball."

10.3   Defenders must "support the cover on the ball."

10.4   Defending players must constantly "adjust their positioning as the ball moves."

COMPETITIVE GAME

10.5   Defenders who pressure the ball need to "drop back immediately after the attacker passes the ball" in order to fill in the space behind them and provide cover or support.

10.6   Until the ball is passed, a defender "should not give up pressuring the ball" until called off by another defender.

10.7   Defenders should not tackle the ball unless "100% certain of winning the ball."

POSITIONAL GAME

10.8   The two lines of defense should "move together."

10.9   Defenders need to "adjust" their positions as the attacking play changes, stepping up when the ball is passed away from the goal and dropping off when a through ball is possible.

10.10   The defense, especially the goalkeeper, should "communicate" about where the defensive line should move.

10.11   The defenders need to "block shots" without overcommitting and letting the attacker dribble past.

10.12   The defenders need to "clear the ball high, wide, and far."

STANDARD GAME

10.13   Players "interchange positions" to create two defensive lines of four.

10.14   The defensive players need to "double up in deep, wide areas" to stop crosses.

ELEMENT #11—DEFENDING: PRESSING

TECHNICAL AND TACTICAL DEVELOPMENT

11.1   Players must "react quickly" to changes in the game.

11.2   Players must "make sharp turns" when changing directions.

COMPETITIVE GAME

11.3   Press the ball to "cut out passing lanes" and "force attackers toward support."

11.4   The defenders need to "press together" to win the ball back.

POSITIONAL GAME

11.5   The attacking players need to "press as a team" to win the ball back quickly.

STANDARD GAME

11.6   Decide "when to press and when to drop off" into a block-zonal defense.

CPS TEAM PROGRESS RATING FORM

Developed by Michael Curless

DATE: _____ TEAM: _____ RATER: _____

Watch your team play a standard game:

1. Team Baseline   Circle what the team performs without coaching interventions.
2. Team Potential   Put a check mark by what the team performs after a reminder.
3. Team Needs   Items left unmarked.

Phase of Play	Objective #1 Create Formation	Objective #2 Primary Movements	Objective #3 Secondary Movements	Objective #4 Transition to the Next Phase
Build-Up	Players spread out to "make the field bigger" after the team wins possession of the ball in their defensive half.	Players pass around pressure using deep angles of support. Players check to the ball and use half-turns to create forward-passing options.	Defenders make passes directly to the forwards when not able to pass around or through the opponent.	After reaching the halfway line, the team looks to attack the goal directly. If attacking directly is not possible, players move into the attacking half in order to probe.
Probing	The team is positioned with several players around the ball in the attacking half (Rondo formation) with one player wide.	The team uses 1- and 2-touch passing combinations and quick turns to keep possession in the attacking half.	The team passes to a wide player away from pressure when the team cannot go directly to goal.	Players recognize when to attack the goal (1v1, overloads) and when to maintain possession.
Attacking	Players attack spaces by dribbling at the opponent and making runs behind them.	Players use 1v1 dribbling moves, wall passes, and through balls to get behind the defense.	Players cross the ball in front of the goal to runners in the penalty box.	Players take hard shots on goal. Players follow up shots for rebounds.
Block-Zonal Defending	Players pressure, cover, and support in a block-zonal formation.	Players win tackles, block shots, and clear the ball with volleys and headers.	Defenders drop back to take away through balls, step up to take away attacking space, and double up wingers.	Players counterattack or keep possession after winning the ball.
Pressing	After losing possession, players nearest the ball press the opponent as a group.	Players cut out passing lanes while swarming the ball.	Defensive players anticipate the long pass from the opponent being pressed and step in front of the attackers to win the ball.	The team directly attacks the goal or keeps possession after winning the ball. The team transitions to a block-zonal formation if not able to win the ball quickly.

Game Notes: _____

_____

_____

ADVANCED NEUROMUSCULAR TRAINING FOR INSTEP SHOOTING

More experienced players can often use more intensive neuromuscular training to break poor shooting habits. The most common mistake is for players to strike the ball with the upper part of the instep with the toe pointed outward and the heel low, creating a wedge with the foot, leading to the ball going high in the air. In youth players, a high shot will often end up landing in the goal, but as players get stronger this technique frequently leads to the ball sailing over the goal.

In advanced neuromuscular training, a resistance band is used to hold the player's foot in the correct shooting position while the kicking foot is off the ground in the open skill position. The resistance band allows the foot to essentially be "grounded" while held in the air because the band helps hold the foot in place in the same way keeping the foot on the ground can help hold the foot position.

"GROUNDED" OPEN SKILL POSITION

A. The player's helper puts a firm resistance band around the kicking foot of the player and holds on to the opposite end behind the player. (The player can also put one end of the resistance band around a stationary object like a goalpost in order to do these exercises alone.)

B. The player lifts the kicking foot in the air and holds the foot in the instep kicking position. The resistance applied to the kicking foot by the band helps the player gain better control over the foot.

C. "Point the kicking foot straight down. It should be a bit more than one stretched hand-width away from your planting foot. The kicking toe should be even with the toe of the planting foot. Crunch at the core, so your body is over the kicking foot with both knees slightly bent. Your kicking foot should be straight up and down, with the knee slightly turned inward so the front of your instep is facing straight ahead." The player should remain in this "grounded" open skill position until the shaking in the kicking foot stops.

D. The player should slowly move the lower kicking leg forward and backward in a shooting motion with the helper applying appropriate resistance to the foot so the band stays taut. Do this exercise until the player is able to keep the foot locked in the correct position while moving it back and forth.

E. The player now snaps the foot forward quickly while the foot is under tension from the band. The helper can adjust to the swinging leg to ensure the same pressure through the swing.

F. Once the player can snap the foot quickly and correctly with resistance, the player needs to practice the shooting motion without the resistance band. If the player is able to hold the foot in the correct position while making the kicking motion without resistance, say, doing instep passing with a partner, then the player can shoot on goal. Shooting on goal will demonstrate how well the neuromuscular training was able to correct old shooting habits and solidify the new shooting foot position.

G. Based on the results of shooting on goal, more neuromuscular training with resistance bands might be appropriate.

STEP-BY-STEP SOCCER SKILL DEVELOPMENT

Step-by-step skill development is important for player success in a standard game. Listed next are variations that you can use to incrementally add game-like pressure to drills.

1. Practice the skill without a ball
   *Players perform neuromuscular training.
2. Practice the skill with a ball
   *Players do the skills while standing in one spot.
3. Practice the skill with a ball and movement
   *Players perform the skills moving around an open area.
4. Practice the skill with a ball, movement, and stationary obstacles
   *Players perform skills in a restricted space: passing patterns and dribbling through cones.
5. Practice the skill with a ball, movement, stationary obstacles, and indirect pressure
   *Players perform skills with player interference: players dribble or partners pass to each other in a restricted space among other players doing the same skills.
6. Practice the skill with a ball, movement, stationary obstacles, and competition
   *Players play a skills-focused game.
7. Practice the skill with a ball, movement, stationary obstacles, competition, and direction
   *Players play a game with goals.
8. Practice the skill with a ball, movement, stationary obstacles, competition, direction, on a regular field
   *Players play a standard game.

REFERENCES

Basile, Pasquale. 2015. *Coaching Positional Play: "Expansive Football" Attacking Tactics & Practices.* London: SoccerTutor.com

Bordonau, Juan, and Jose Villanueva. 2018. *Tactical Periodization: A Proven Successful Training Model.* London: SoccertTutor.com

Coyle, Daniel. 2009. *The Talent Code.* London: Arrow Books

Cruyff, Johan. 2016. *My Turn: A Life of Total Football.* New York: Nation Books

Goncalves, Jose. 1998. *The Principles of Brazilian Soccer.* Spring City: Reedswain Books

Gray, Andy. 2000. *Flat Back Four: The Tactical Game.* Spring City: Reedswain Inc

Honigstein, Raphael. 2015. *Das Reboot.* New York: Nation Books

Honigstein, Raphael. 2018. *Bring the Noise.* New York: Nation Books

James, William. 1918. *The Principles of Psychology.* New York: Henry Holt and Company

Jankowski, Timo. 2016. *Coaching Soccer like Guardiola and Mourinho.* Aachen: Meyer & Meyer

Tamarit, Xavier. 2014. *What is Tactical Periodization?* Oakamoor: Bennion Kearny Limited

Meijer, Maarten. 2006. *Guus Hiddink: Going Dutch.* Milsons Point: Random House

Meijer, Maarten. 2014. *Louis Van Gaal: The Biography.* Ebury Press

Michels, Rinus. 2001. *Team Building: The Road to Success.* Spring City: Reedswain Publishing

Perarnau, Marti. 2016. *Pep Guardiola: The Evolution.* Edinburgh: Arena Sport

Syed, Matthew. 2010. *Bounce.* New York: HarperCollins Publishers

Whitehouse, Matthew. 2014. *Universality: The Blueprint for Soccer's New Era.* Oakamoor: Bennion Kearny Limited

Winter, Henry. 2014. *Pep Confidential.* Edinburgh: Arena Sport

CREDITS

Cover and interior design: Hannah Park

Layout: DiTech Publishing Services, www.ditechpubs.com

Cover and chapter opener photos: © AdobeStock

Drill diagrams: © www.academysoccercoach.co.uk

Illustrations: Raina Taseva

Managing editor: Elizabeth Evans

Copyeditor: Stephanie Kramer